Interplay

Contemplations on Creativity

By Michael J. Vaughn

For Gabriele Rico

Introduction

I was always going to be a novelist. The question was, what were my novels going to be *about*? Looking back, it's clear that I never really had a choice.

It all began when Maurice Jackson told me I wasn't cool enough to be in the men's glee club. Seriously. Peterson High was like a Disney musical. Men's glee had 125 members, including half the football team. We sang like gorillas, occasionally like dogs. We rewrote "Winter Wonderland" into a celebration of sex, drugs and booze ("…to face unafraid, the chicks that we laid…"). But we also toured other schools, encouraging boys to sing. And we once had to postpone a playoff game because the entire baseball team was playing baseball players in *Damn Yankees*.

I went to college at San Jose State largely because it was close to home - and proceeded to klutz my way into a world-class choir. Our first performance was in San Francisco's brand-new Davies Symphony Hall, and we sang on a regular basis with the San Jose Symphony, including a memorable Beethoven's Ninth. The department also had a gamelan ensemble that performed with composer Lou Harrison, a young jazz instructor named Bobby McFerrin, and Irene Dalis, a twenty-year star of the Metropolitan Opera who had returned to her hometown to start an opera workshop.

As a singing journalism major, I wrote about these things for the *Spartan Daily*, and I also received some tickets from the San Francisco Opera for a touring production of Verdi's *Rigoletto*. The performance had two intriguing angles: Mark Rucker, a black Rigoletto (at a time when colorblind casting was still a new concept) and a third-act storm scene that benefited from actual thunder and lightning just outside the semi-covered Concord Pavilion. The subsequent review – plus an interview with Rucker – won that semester's award for best arts feature.

It was becoming apparent that I had the specific ability to *write* about *music*. This is not a talent to be overlooked. Music is ruthlessly temporary, existing only in the present, as difficult to pin down as a butterfly on speed. "Writing about music," says a quote attributed to just about everyone, "is like dancing about furniture." (Reflecting this difficulty, the last thing the average music magazine addresses is the actual *music*.) On the bright side, music is endlessly diverse, forever fascinating, and the challenge of describing it never lessens.

And still, even after I decided to write about it, music stalked me. The year I graduated, Irene Dalis's workshop became Opera San Jose, and Silicon Valley's new weekly, *Metro*, needed someone to cover it. *Metro*'s jazz writer, Sammy Cohen, sold me a used drum kit, sparking a journey through a dozen jazz, blues and rock bands, plus one memorable drum circle. A local arts center, Villa Montalvo, needed a publicist – preferably someone who could *write* about *music* – for its 50-concert arts season. I emceed performances, escorted Harry Connick, Jr.'s fiancee, rapped backstage with Jon Hendricks, introduced my dad to his idol, Al Hirt, and appeared over Charlie Sheen's shoulder in a Clint Eastwood movie.
With all this raw material beating me over the head, it was no surprise when my first novels featured artist protagonists. My first, *Frozen Music*, took place in a college choir. My next two – accepted by separate publishers in one very memorable week – featured a young opera singer (*Gabriella's Voice*) and a theater center modeled after Villa Montalvo (*Courting the Seventh Sister*).

Thirteen novels on, I am still drawing from the well – poets, drummers, painters, composers, jazz singers, actors – and I am still thirsty. But it's not just a matter of harvesting themes like an arborist picking fruit. There's something more dynamic at work. Every time I pick up a pair of drumsticks, begin a painting, sing a Sinatra tune or review an opera, I give my internal turbine a spin, creating new energy for my fiction.

Beginning in 2005, the editors of *Writer's Digest* handed me a number of assignments that challenged me to explain this and other phenomena surrounding the creative act. "Creative Lollygagging" describes the act of finding inspiration by not seeking it. In "Vice-Versa," three noted authors describe the divine interplay between poetry and prose. The culmination is "Meeting of the Minds," an exploration of the visual-linguistic synergy between the left and right hemispheres of the brain.

Encouraged by WD's reprinting of these articles, most recently in a book-length collection of fiction writing, I began to visualize a book that would bring all of my worlds together, a collection of articles, short stories, novel excerpts and poems reflecting a quarter-century study of the creative act. For dessert, I have included quotes from some of the artists I've had the pleasure of interviewing along the way. My attempt to sort these pieces into discrete categories lasted perhaps five minutes. I have opted instead for a subtle narrative thread, a trick I learned from my friend Calder Lowe, masterful editor of *The Montserrat Review*.

I hope that you will find in these pieces the same entertainment, fascination and creative spark that I found in the artists who inspired them. I have had a hell of a lot of fun.

Instructions for Finding Frosted Glass at the Beach

The glass is commonly found in the middle rocks
at the edge of the high- tide wash
an hour before sunset in fall
when the waves are beginning to churn

Walk easy, look hard, but
not so hard that you can't hear the ocean

The best are found alone
on plains of wet sand teased by the breakers
Keep your gaze to the sun and
watch for them flashing
guitar- pick chinks of white, green, brown
the rare and lovely blue
stitching your pockets, scraping as you walk

Take five minutes to watch the sun fall away
This will cost you the green and the brown
which will turn in the gloaming to coal-dark lumps
but the clear is still a possibility
even, occasionally, in moonlight
as long as you ignore the luminescent impostor
the triangular fragment of shell

Remember that your quarry lies in a middle ground
that these fallen stars come not from
beauty but from someone
throwing litter on a beach

Do not feel the need to restock
this will be done for you.

First published in *Parting Gifts*
Greensboro, North Carolina

"To me, singing is all about getting out of your voice's way. We all like to have control over our voices, but it's precisely in giving up control that your voice has its own freedom."
--Rochelle Bard, opera singer

Creative Lollygagging

Experiencing Writer's Block? Maybe you need to work harder on working less.

First published in Writer's Digest

Perhaps the biggest mistake that writers make is thinking that they can sit down in front of a notebook or computer screen and wait for ideas to simply show up.

Nope. You'd better have some ideas *before* you sit down, and you'd better figure out a system for harvesting those ideas.

You can start by thinking of yourself as a satellite dish. The way that a dish receives signals is a decidedly passive activity, but nothing comes in until the equipment is properly charged and opened to the universe.

A few years ago, ensconced in one of my "brewing" modes – done with my last novel, waiting for the next to come a-knockin' – I decided to take my dish to the beach and open 'er up.

About a half-mile along, I noticed a friendly spark among the small rocks, and found bits of frosted glass – triangular shards worn to a gem-like smoothness by sand and wave. I remembered the fascination I felt as a child – that nature could take a piece of manmade litter and make it so beautiful. I walked a little farther, discovered another smattering, and had the following thought: *What if someone became so obsessed with frosted glass that he decided to make it his life's work?*

I didn't know it yet, but the satellite dish had just taken in an entire novel.

But not just that. It also took in the process for *imagining* a novel. In the following months, as I continued my beach hikes in search of frosted glass (if my character was obsessed, *I* had to be obsessed), I discovered an intriguing pattern. I arrived at the beach between chapters (my characters dangling in mid-air, awaiting their instructions); I left with pocketfuls of glass *and* my next chapter, nicely mapped out in my head.

It began to seem, in fact, that my novel was scattered along the beach, like pirate's treasure, and all I had to do was come along and scoop it up. The real secret, however, came from my protagonist, Frosted Glass Man, as he was helping a neophyte who had lost her "glass vision."

"Let me guess," he said. "Suddenly you can't tell frosted glass from the Queen of England, and you're sort of losing your place on the sand. Feeling disoriented."

"Yeah. That about describes it."

He grinned. "You're trying too hard. When you begin to lose your sight, just rub the last piece you found, and listen to the ocean."

In other words, if you subtly stimulate your other senses – in this case, tactile (the glass) and auditory (the ocean) – you can take the "edge" away from your conscious, purposive mind, return the satellite dish to a state of active passivity, and open yourself to the forces of serendipidity. And if you come to the beach for frosted glass, you'll also get ideas for your story, slipping in along your peripheral vision.

A Definition

So what makes lollygagging *creative* lollygagging? Let's look at the basic elements:

Activity: We are *not* talking about sitting around on a couch. Just as a satellite dish needs electricity, you need some blood pumping into that brain.

Low Focus: Neither should the activity be so intense that you don't have time to think (Grand Prix and ice hockey are out). Look for a mellow pursuit, surrounded by low-level distractions.

Separation: If you don't hie thee away from the computer, the TV, the bills and the kid, you're headed for a mighty wall o' brainlock.

May We Suggest…

Mobile (because it's hard to preoccupy a moving target): biking, hiking, kayaking, Rollerblading, a long road or train trip.

Idle Pursuits: fly-fishing, horseshoe-tossing, kite-flying, a solo game of eight-ball (loser buys), a solo game of bowling (winner buys), a session at the batting cage or driving range.

Boring Jobs (for those who simply must *be productive):* paint the garage, rake the leaves, pressure-wash the deck, clean out the roof gutters, mow the lawn.

Dilletanting (only effective if you try something for which you have absolutely no talent): abstract painting, composing chance music on the piano, creating monsters from modeling clay, inventing a ballet to your favorite symphony, pounding on a conga drum.

The Coffeehouse Ritual

If you'd like to take this one step further, try combining your lollygagging with your writing ritual. The Coffeehouse Ritual is a routine I've followed for 15 years, with excellent results (in fact, I used it to write this story).

Pick Ur Place: Locate a coffeehouse a mile or two from your home (ideally, a 30-45 minute walk).

The Walk-Up: Head off at an easy pace (no power-walking, please) and let your thoughts drift. For the first few blocks, you'll likely be occupied by small matters of the day. Don't worry – this is a necessary step, one that will clear out your mind for the work ahead. As you pass the halfway point, your thoughts should turn naturally to the project at hand.

Write! Buy something large and sippable, find a non-jiggling table and go to it. Note: keep your coffeehouse sacred. Be polite but not excessively friendly to baristas and regulars. If a friend drops by, tell them that you have five minutes to talk, but then you really need to get back to work. If they're not buying it, tell them you're on deadline.

The Walk-Down: The hike back home is often the most rewarding part of the process. Still adrift on your creative buzz, you may find that your satellite dish is more open than ever. It's a great time to think about what you've just written, and to contemplate future developments.

The Lollygagging Habits of Successful Writers

Tanya Shaffer, playwright, *Baby Taj*

"Before I was a mama,… I would just get in the car and drive for a while and see where I ended up. Out of that came a habit of staying a few days at the Motel 6 in Petaluma."

Mary Bracken Phillips, lyricist/playwright, *The Haunting of Winchester*

"I walk with my dogs (one Australian shepherd and one border collie) on the Croton Aqueduct, a real old road in the woods. And a lyric I was stuck on is suddenly there."

Jane Hirshfield, poet, *After* (HarperCollins)

"When I'm actually working on a poem, I often do something I think of after the fact as 'taking it for a walk.' That is, once I've reached a certain stage of revision, I set the poem aside and go walking – but the poem often starts saying itself in my mind – often with new ideas for revisions, additions, changes."

Frosted Glass Woman

In the novel *Frosted Glass* (Dead End Street, LLC), Sandy Lowiltry meets Frosted Glass Man, a handsome eccentric who spends his days harvesting sea glass on the beaches of Oregon. Frosty attributes the power of the glass to a pseudo-religious figure he calls Frosted Glass Woman. When Sandy asks him to explain this to her, he offers the following story.

Far away, in the birthplace of music and strawberries, there lived a race of beings with skins of glass. Not the brittle, breakable glass of Earth, but a kind of self-contained fluid, a substance that could heal almost immediately after being scratched or punctured. Their organs were made of metals – soft, living versions of silver, copper and titanium. In order to hide these organs from view, the skin had developed an opaque, frosted appearance, much like Earth glass that has been tumbled in the ocean.

Because of these differences in their physical makeup, these glasslings lived much longer than humans, and were a highly evolved, creative race. Their greatest creativity came from their women, whose powers reached their peak during a psycho-physiological phenomenon known as a "blossomfire." Considered events of great awe and mystery, blossomfires would begin appearing in glass women at the age of maturity – about a thousand Earth years – and would cease at the age of reverence, around 4,300 years. Blossomfires usually appeared every 200 years, and lasted only a few Earth days – in glassling terms, a very brief period. Occasionally, however, there came a glass woman who carried the capacity for much lengthier blossomfires; one who was able to cultivate heightened powers and ever-expanding levels of creativity.

Just such a being was Frosted Glass Woman, who for purposes of this telling we will call "Sandy." Sandy's first blossomfire lasted for three of our weeks. As she matured into young womanhood under the tutelage of a woman of reverence we shall call "Lowiltry," her blossomfires lengthened into months and years, and her creative ventures grew ever larger and more complex. Her first was a process for distilling the elements of individual personalities into the form of perfumes. Her second was a kind of jewelry that changed shape and color according to the direction, and intensity of a person's gaze. Another time, she invented a form of music that she called "jazz," but she had no idea what to do with it.

Nearing an age of 3,000 Earth years, Sandy realized that her powers were coming to a peak. For her next blossomfire, she settled on an unprecedented project: the creation of her own world. Her mentor, Lowiltry, warned against this. A project this expansive would extend Sandy's blossomfire to dangerous lengths. Those attempting this kind of extension before had fallen into a state the glasslings referred to as "the hardening," in which the fluid glass of the skin becomes hard and fragile like the glass of Earth. The condition lasted for a thousand years, during which time the victim had to be hung by wires over a bed of snowy egret feathers.

Shortly after this warning, however, Lowiltry was overcome by a sudden illness and began to rapidly deteriorate. At the very start of her student's Great Blossomfire, she passed away, her elements rising to the sky in banners of copper, silver and white vapor. Spying this sad but lovely vision as she entered her creative trance, Sandy was more determined than ever to achieve her ends, if only as a tribute to her mentor.

Dipping a hand into the glassling world's still-molten third moon, Sandy drew out a sphere of hot elements and blew it cool with her breath. As the crust began to harden, she drew canyons and mountains with her fingers, and then outlined long gouges and wide depressions that she filled with her tears. She plucked out strands of her hair and formed them into trees, plants and seaweed, then molded small bits of the crust into mammals, fish and birds, animating them with drops of perspiration. She also found places for her previous inventions. The perfume she swept into the hearts of a million flowers. The jewelry she deposited just under the surface, where they awaited the wandering gaze, the searching hands. As for jazz, she hid that in the trunk of a tree on the plains of Africa.

Sandy completed her hew world just as she felt her Great Blossomfire ending. But her creation was missing something, and she knew that this was something not even she could produce: living spirits, souls, intellects, sparks of self-knowledge. She felt great sadness, for what good was this new world of hers without some form of cognizant being to behold, observe and admire its beauty?

By the time she came to terms with her defeat, it was too late – the hardening had begun. Sandy felt great, sudden terror, not at the physical reality of her petrifying skin, but at the thought of spending year upon year suspended by wires as her creation sat there with no knowledge of its own existence.

Stumbling along on her stiffening limbs, Sandy drew herself down a path behind her home to the top of a great sea cliff. By the time she approached the edge, she could move only her left arm. But this was enough. With painful effort she pulled her green arms and face, her white torso and brown legs alongside the drop. She lifted her blue eyes in a final prayer to Lowiltry, then pushed off as her arm froze into place. Frosted Glass Woman hurtled avenues of air and fell to the rocks, smashing her skin into a million pieces.

Aware of their daughter's wishes, Sandy's bereaved parents spent the next three hundred years roaming the shoreline, gathering the pieces of their daughter's skin and scattering them over her newly created world. As the pieces became more and more difficult to find, and finally disappeared completely, her father became overwhelmed by grief. One morning, in a burst of anger, he picked up his daughter's world and hurled it into the vast recesses of space. The new world settled into orbit around a small, stable sun, and the pieces of glass took physical form, becoming that which we call women.

To this day, Frosted Glass Man wanders the shorelines of Earth, hoping one day to reassemble Frosted Glass Woman and bring her back to life.

In your poetry, you make great use of surreal imagery. Do you have a hard time getting your students to take similar "flights" in their work?

"They are not used to using imagination. Most have plenty of it, but they are embarrassed by it, so my job is to convince them it's all about taking chances, risking making a fool of oneself and going for broke. Otherwise, why write?"
  --Charles Simic, poet

Precipitous

Long before I intellectualized
the world into a
windstorm of rods and cones
I recall

standing in the rain
watching a slick of oil as it
snakes down the gutter like a
long, liquid cypress tree

Framing the surface to a
lunchbox-size lake,
I spot a single pockmark landing and
reverse the telescope

winding it back on a
kitestring to the clouds
where it balances in the vapor like an
English riding champion
waiting for gravity to deliver its
unassailable marching orders

Around the corner my gutterstream
breaks loose, a centrifugal fan
fingering the asphalt for flaws and seams
tracking south to an unseen ocean

I picture myself on a beach
six months later.
I spy my single drop on a
sea lion's nose and exclaim,
"Friend! How are you?
You're looking well."

At what height did I stop
watching the rain?
Five-two? Four-foot-eight?

Short enough only today, only now
to set aside my junk mail
see a thing for a thing and
inventory the small dramas at my feet.

First published in Terrain.org

Meeting of the Minds

Get your bossy, literal-minded left brain in touch with its more creative counterpart.

First published in Writer's Digest

When I was a teen, I asked my mother if I could clip a rose from her garden to give to a date. "Sure," she said. "In fact, the more roses you clip, the more the plant produces."

I've carried this metaphor around ever since, and thought of it recently when I noticed something about my paintings. Rather than "sapping" my creative juices, my afternoons at the canvas actually *increased* the energy and vividness of subsequent writing sessions. I began to wonder if there was something going on in my brain that would account for this cross-pollenation – and if this was something that other writers could use to invigorate their creative powers. The answer is a resounding yes, and it has everything to do with being in your right mind – at the right time.

Hemispheric Diplomacy

In the 1970s, neuroscientist Roger Sperry conducted studies on epileptics who had undergone "split-brain" operations – a severing of the corpus callosum, the bundle of nerve fibers that connects the two hemispheres of the cerebral cortex. The studies revealed remarkable differences in the ways that the two hemispheres process the world. The left operates in a linear fashion, piecing things together in a logical, sequential assembly of parts; it also contains the mind's center for language skills (both written and spoken) and calculation. The right hemisphere operates through images, concepts and patterns; it possesses a much higher capacity for ambiguity and complexity, as well as a special aptitude for spatial relationships.

Sperry's conclusions found an immediate place in popular culture; people began calling themselves "right-brainers" and "left-brainers" in the same way that one would say "Virgo" or "Republican." Artists tend to jump on the right-brain bandwagon, which – especially for writers – can be an egregious misnomer (remember those left-brain language skills?).

In her 2004 book, *An Alchemy of Mind*, science-poet Diane Ackerman writes, "Mind isn't a tug-of-war with the left brain on one side and the right brain on the other, but a collaboration, an open exchange."

Thus, the secret for the creative writer is not to lean inordinately on one hemisphere or the other, but to manipulate the lively conversation going on *between* the hemispheres, through the corpus callosum.

In her 1983 book, *Writing the Natural Way*, Dr. Gabriele Rico brought Sperry's findings to the field of creative writing through the practice of "clustering." The writer develops an idea by writing a "nucleus" word, circling it, then quickly writing associated words around it, circling them, and drawing lines that connect back to the nucleus. The neat mental trick that this resultant spiderweb performs is to take words – generally under the purview of the left brain – and turn them into a piece of visual art, which taps into the pattern-seeking abilities of the right brain. And *that* is where innovation comes from.

"It is the right brain that processes all novel stimuli," says Rico. "Whereas the left brain simply tunes it out. Any idea or exciting thought about character or plot has got to come through the right brain, because the left brain only recognizes what it has already learned."

The biggest obstacle in the creative process comes from the left brain, which, with its flair for logic and its ceaseless yakking, is well-equipped to be bossy and overbearing. In a wacky family sitcom we'll call *Meet the Brainers*, little Roger Right Brainer is a shy but imaginative daydreamer type, filled with ideas. Anytime he tries to express one of them, however, his literal-minded big sister, Lucy Left Brainer, says, "Oh, that's just stupid," or "What have *you* been smoking?"

The secret of clustering is to get Lucy to just *shut up* for a second and listen to Roger's idea. The thing is, however, you're going to need Lucy eventually, because at a terribly exciting moment that Rico calls the "trial-web shift," you will identify the pattern contained within that cluster and need to call up those left-brain language skills in order to pin it down on paper.

"Risking an analogy," writes Rico, "I might say that your (right) mind attends to the melody of life, whereas your (left) mind attends to the notes that compose the melody. And here is the key to natural writing: The melodies must come first."

Child's Play

"It takes a long time to become young again."
--Picasso

Most creators know that a child-like sense of play is an essential element of the artistic process, but many may not be aware of the very real scientific basis for this idea. In early childhood, the corpus callosum is non-functioning, allowing the two hemispheres to develop independently. This great plasticity of mind allows infants to gobble up the world around them in large chunks, and to make associations in a highly imaginative, playful right-brain fashion. It also allows them to inhale language like little linguistic geniuses.

The hemispheres begin to specialize at age five, when most children have mastered speech. The corpus callosum achieves full function between the ages of nine and 12, and the left brain takes over with a vengeance. Suddenly that kid who used to draw purple grass and blue suns turns into a literal-minded peer conformist. The pattern is reinforced by an educational system with a decided left-brain bias (the best creative minds tend to score a rather pedestrian 120 to 130 on the IQ test), and a lot of people just get stuck there.

Like me. For 20 years, I gave up on visual art, because I couldn't "draw" – that is, take an object from real life and reproduce it on paper. One night, I found myself at a restaurant with paper tablecloths and crayons, and began to draw random lines that intersected like roads on a map. When I began to see the outlines of faces, I applied eyes, noses and mouths, and suddenly I had a place setting of fantastical creatures from some sneaky, playful menagerie in my brain. Five years later, they've made their way onto large acrylic paintings, hanging on the walls of a coffeehouse in Tacoma. Naturally, they draw comparisons to Picasso, who seems to represent the playful, child-like artist in all of us.

Striking a Balance

So. Have I found the answer to my original question? Almost. In his 2001 book, *Mozart's Brain and the Fighter Pilot*, neuropsychiatrist Richard Restak, M.D. posits the notion that the most effective brain is the one that achieves the best balance between the hemispheres. Consider your own writing sessions. Isn't it much easier to focus while listening to instrumental music? That's because song lyrics tap into the same left-brain language center you're trying to use for your novel or poem, and jam up the works.

"As a practical application of your new knowledge of cerebral geography," Restak writes, "look for ways of combating mental fatigue by switching to activities that use different parts of the brain."

You probably do this already. When you're writing, and you're feeling tired, don't you look up from the page and gaze at some distant object? You're not just resting your eyes, you're resting your left brain, by switching over to the right brain for a brief study of pattern and color. If you perform the same action when you're searching for your next line, or looking for just the right word, you may be using that lamp or painting or barista (or the silver sedan I've been staring at for 20 seconds now) as a catalyst for your conceptual right-brain idea factory.

If you're paying attention, you may now be experiencing a "trial-web shift." (Feel free to say "Aha!" or "Eureka!") If an author uses pattern play and visual imagery to find that next line, could he not use a couple hours of painting as a way of "priming the pump" for a writing session? Dr. Rico?

"Absolutely," says Dr. Rico. "And people who don't spend any time in the spatial realm of images will never get to prime the pump."

Reinforcing this image-idea connection is the way that so many authors receive major plot-turns as mental Polaroids. Rico cites a recent interview with author Joan Didion, who says that she begins her novels with nothing more than a single visual image. The final scene of my own work-in-progress also arrived in this package – a freeze-frame of two former lovers meeting unexpectedly on a dance floor. How did they get there? What happens next? My left and right brains will just have to grapple with each other until we figure that out.

All of which brings us to softball (no, really). My best writing sessions of all come after my Wednesday slow-pitch league, when I adjourn to a café across the street and write my little head off. Which now makes perfect sense. Not only does a softball game flood your brain with oxygen, it's an hour-long bonanza of pattern assessment and spatial study (consider the complex judgements involved in chasing down a fly ball, or striking a round ball with a round stick). Then, after writing, I decompress by playing pinball – yet another study of pattern, motion and space. As it turns out, my Wednesdays nights are a veritable, er, tennis match of left- and right-brain activities.

The Mind 2.0

Frankly, everything you've read on these pages is highly simplified; the brain is too marvelous and complex to contain in this modest article. But I hope I've given you a few ways for your brain to know itself. Perhaps the most important lesson of all is to know that your brain is an organism that is designed to redesign itself. If you're feeling stuck, you don't have to stay that way.

An astounding example of this comes from one of our experts, Diane Ackerman. Ackerman's partner, Paul West, author of some 45 non-fiction books, suffered a stroke three years ago that left him aphasic – unable to speak, write, understand or even process language.

"But his *creativity* remained intact," says Ackerman, "to be expressed in words, despite his loss of the language areas." After "a colossal daily effort on his part, and mine, to recruit other areas of the brain for language use… he's written an aphasic memoir (due out next year), short stories, a novel, and he's midway through a second novel."

Getting Into Your Right Mind

Whether you use them to develop a specific idea, or just to shake up the ol' corpus callosum, the following are great games of "fetch" for your conceptualizing right brain.

The Classic Rico Cluster

Write a word. Circle it. Write an associated word nearby. Circle that word, and draw a line back to the original word. Keep going, building up a spiderweb of word-associations, until you see a pattern. When the "trial-web shift" hits, you'll be dying to write it into an essay, story or poem.

Cagean Chance Operations

To achieve true randomness, stated composer-philosopher John Cage, ya gotta have a plan. Pick out your favorite book, go to every tenth page and write down the first full word on that page. Study your list of random words and see if any patterns come out. Nothing doing? Pick out your favorite and use it to start a cluster.

The Vaughnean Doodle

Draw a series of random lines that intersect like roads on a map (don't think too much). When they begin to assume shapes, throw in some universal facial elements: eyes, mouth, ears, nose. Now study the creature you've created and write down who he is, what he's been doing, how he's feeling – or just use him as the main character in a story.

The Amazing Technicolor Dreambook

Keep a notepad and pen on your nightstand. Immediately upon waking, write down anything you can remember from your dreams. None of it has to make sense – this is just your right brain's way of processing the day's memories.

A Note: I was fortunate enough to work as a student assistant in the English Department at San Jose State when Dr. Gabriele Rico was teaching there, enjoying the success of her 1983 best-seller, *Writing the Natural Way*. Dr. Rico died of cancer in early 2013, and the world is a lot less interesting for her departure.

"You don't *have* to understand everything you see. Look for something you can relate to. It's just taking you on a journey to places you haven't been before. *That's* the important part."
  --Margaret Wingrove, choreographer

The Train to Unattainia

I inhabit the space inside the wall
after the flip of the switch but before
the dark of the bulb

I am a ruthless cowboy semicolon
forever inserting myself into conversations
riding the hum of the intermission
crowd like a sailor, tying silk scarves around
their slow-nodding heads and

running
the rise of the curtain my only ticket in.

The only breath I take (breathe)
comes on the twentieth mile (breathe)
of a thousand-mile drive
when I know that turning around is no longer an option
sunshine blowing through the vents like
powdered sugar

I go to the land where nothing can be had
running down a long hard ribbon of willful disconnect
a palpable lack of direction.

The needle winds its way in and out of the continental fabric
pulling me along to Cheyenne, Wyoming
where my siren, Improvisia
stands upright on a green sidewalk

In one hand she holds a book of songs
in the other a bucket of blue paint
dips the one in the other till the
color bleeds out the notes

She hands it to me with an Andalusian smile and says
Here, it's the one you asked for
Open it up and
sing, baby, sing

First published in di-verse-city
Austin, Texas

The Secret Daughter of Apollo

In the novel *Gabriella's Voice* (Dead End Street, LLC), opera aficionado Bill Harness offers encouragement both personal and financial to a young Seattle soprano, Gabriella Compton. When her new patron begins to demonstrate some unstable behavior, however, Gabriella demands an explanation.

I took her to Fort Ward, on the south tip of the island, where they have old cannon placements from World War Two, designed to guard the entrance to the Bremerton Shipyards (they were never used). The cannons are no longer there, just the big concrete placements, with stairs leading down to tiny shelters. We were walking on the lawn next to them when Gabriella let out one of her involuntary songbursts. There was something moving in the grass.

"Don't worry," I said. "It's just a garter snake. Nothing harmful."

"Are you sure?"

"Yep. I used to have one when I was a kid." I took a big step toward our new friend and he slithered off under a hedge, a four-foot, dark green rope.

"Well," she said. "I'm glad you know your reptiles. Are we almost there? I have to be back for rehearsal at noon."

"Uh-huh. Sure. Over this way."

I took her down a path curving through tall hedges like an English labyrinth. Fifty feet on we took a sharp right, passed through a couple of pleasantly grassy waterbanks, then turned left onto a clearing edged in tangles of blackberry vines. At the end of the clearing was a white wooden belvedere looking out over the dark waters of Rich Passage.

"Ooh!" said Gabriella. "D'you suppose they're ripe?"

"They're a little picked over, but I think you'll find a few. Be careful, though. If they're not real dark, chances are they'll be a little..."

"Ooh!"

"Tart." I turned to see Gabriella's lips performing various gymnastics (the uneven parallel bars, the balance beam) trying to drive out the sourness. She popped in two berries of a riper disposition, and this seemed to balance things out.

I entered the belvedere and sat on its gray, windworn bench, looking up to study the vines winding their way in and out of its roof slats. Gabriella settled on the grass a few feet outside, a pyramid of ripe berries balanced in her left hand.

"Is this about... last night?" she asked. "Because you really don't have to..."

"No, I think I do need to explain. You know, at first I took that strange hostility of yours as something resembling normal, everyday jealousy. But when you brought up the yodeling, I think I understood, because you know the moment those notes came out of my mouth in that ferry shelter, I felt guilty about it.

"I'm sure you've figured this out, Rosina, but you and I have sort of a strange friendship – wonderful, but strange, and it seems to be built largely on music. You have given me so much of it, and I have only talked about it, and, also, I've been hesitant to give you any pieces of my past. So you felt betrayed when I revealed a sort of singing talent to someone else."

Gabriella pursed her lips together in a satisfied way. "Exactly," she said.

"And I got some 'splainin' to do."

"Si."

"Well. I'm not really up to yodeling for you just yet, so instead I will give you another piece of my past – a piece that no one on this planet besides yourself will ever receive. I hope you can see the spirit in which I'm giving it. God, I sound like a damn lawyer up here."

Gabriella popped another trio of blackberries in her mouth, turning her tongue to a ripe purple. "So... this is part two."

"Part two."

"Your mother."

"My mother."

She caught the look in my eyes and hesitated. "This isn't easy for you, is it, Billy? I mean, you really don't have to do this. You can save this for later. I'm really over what happened last night and..."

"No," I said. "I think I need to get a little tougher about things like this. If I keep saving my little stories up for later I might blow up someday. Maybe my traumas need to be a little more... casual." I looked around for something to do with my hands. There was a square of latticework at the side of the belvedere, and in the middle of the square was a single red blackberry. I plucked it and threw it in my mouth. It was awfully tart, but the snap of it threw me off for a second and gave me a chance to get started.

"I saw an interview once with a soprano who was doing Madama Butterfly, and they asked her what it was like, having to go out and off herself ever other night. She said, 'It's just nice to be considered important enough to die.'

"My mother spent a lot of time dying. Well that's a strange way to put it. But anyway, my father and she had some sort of secret agreement that she wouldn't sing. I could never quite understand that. I loved my mother's voice; I lived for it. Especially after I'd heard my grandmother sing, after I understood the connection. There was nothing more thrilling to me than listening to my mother sing. And she did sing, agreement or not – there's no way she could stop it. Of course she only say during my father's business trips, so, in a strange way, I looked forward to his absences. And I began to resent him and his silly rules.

"And what glory, about a week after his departure, when my mother's voice began to break its way out of the chrysalis and take over the household. It always took her a few days to warm up, but by the end of that second week she was performing entire scenes for us, acting them out, pouring out that gorgeous lyric soprano like... like.... I always had a hard time coming up with a description for it, but one time in a college English class I came close, in a poem that I wrote for an assignment.

"I wrote that my mother was one of the secret daughters of Apollo, and one long summer day Apollo had became tired of his work and left his chariot high in the heavens while he went to visit his favorite daughter. But he didn't have a gift to bring her, so he caught a meteorite shooting down toward the earth, cracked it in half and hollowed it out to form a goblet. Then he took a single ray of sunshine and squeezed it in his hands until it came out as pineapple juice and dripped into the goblet. He offered the goblet to my mother, and after she drank the juice she could feel the light coursing through her body, and she had only to open her mouth to let bits of it back into the sky as sound – courageous, bronze, tropical sound. I never turned that poem in; I couldn't bear to let it go. I turned in something else and got a C.

"She liked death scenes most of all. Cio-Cio-San. Violetta. Mimi. The slow poisoning of Leonora. The selfless leap of Gilda into Sparafucile's knife. The mournful wasting away of Melisande. The shocking strangulation of Desdemona. She'd set up a mattress next to the kitchen table and perform Tosca leaping from the parapet of the Castel Sant'Angelo.

One summer we had one of those above-ground swimming pools, and she would swim off to the Flying Dutchman's ship, and then ascend to heaven once she reached the other side. Only it was my mother's notion that Senta would not ascend to heaven with a bathing suit on, so halfway across the pool she would take it off, and rise from the far side in the nude. This might have been no big deal, except that old Mr. Shoriff next door was outside mowing his lawn, and nearly had a heart attack."

Gabriella snickered into her hand, then popped in a few more berries, like a kid eating popcorn at the movies. She lifted her eyes skyward and smiled.

"She really, really loved it, didn't she?"

"The opera? Yes. She was born to it. And... I grew fond of watching my mother die.

"And after she was done, she taught my brother Bobby and I to yell 'Brava! Brava! Bravissima!' and to keep clapping until she could make two or three appearances from behind the living room drapes. One day she splurged and bought two dozen long-stem roses so we could toss them at her as she made her deep, humble diva bows. And then, when we had thrown every one, we'd pick them up and do it all over again. My mother was the greatest of the unknown prima donnas.

"After her performances, she was always so hyped up that she would let us stay up late with her and watch great old black-and-white movies, and she'd bake us cookies: peanut butter cookies, oatmeal cookies, ginger snaps, macaroons, lemon bars – and if she had sung really well, chocolate chip cookies.

"The idea of death, in my impressionable ten-year-old mind, became a fascinating and playful thing, and I grew so fond of it that I would take it to school with me. I was constantly dreaming up new ways of killing myself. I would be leaning peacefully against a brick wall when suddenly it would fall on top of me, pinning me to the ground as the remaining bricks fell down one by one, each smashing a different bone as it landed, until I was nothing more than a sheet of pulpy flesh. Or I would trip and fall backward through a window, but I would come out the other side without scratch, just like a hero in an old-fashioned Western – but then, just as I was celebrating my good luck, dusting off my chaps and preparing to go back in the saloon to rejoin the brawl, one last tiny sliver would slip from the window frame and pierce me, with the greatest possible degree of irony and fatality, right in the jugular. Or I would be happily playing on the swing when a sudden gale would blow me over, and my neck would land squarely on the leather strap, and then the wind would spin me around until the strap tightened around my neck and strangled me slowly to death.

"And sure, you know little boys, they make up these kind of things all the time. Watch them play with toy soldiers sometime. But they don't sing thrilling arias as they twist in the wind – and being neither strong of voice nor compositionally attuned, my melodies were not arias so much as rough-cut cascades of whines and moans and shouting. I was sent home several times with a note from the principal suggesting I seek some sort of counseling. And my father would look at my mother in that accusing way, because little boys don't start singing death scenes all by themselves, of course, and that would usually be enough to send my mother into one of her days-long funks.

"Her depressions were generally triggered by conflicts like these – many times just by the guilt she would feel when my father returned from his trips, whether he knew about her singing or not. She was pretty much an invalid during these times, confined to her bed, barely uttering a word or moving a muscle, eating only when it was forced upon her, and completely devoid of any capacity for joy or hope."

Gabriella's eyes were open and bare to me now, so intent I could not quite stand it. I drifted off over the water, scanning the green stripe of Point Glover, and sought out a single spot of blue in the overcast, cut out in the shape of Indiana. I aimed my words directly into it.

"My father had been gone a week. My mother had worked past humming to trilling and I knew I was due for a meal of her tangy Italian diction any day, so I walked quickly home from school. It was spring. I remember, a little drizzle falling in the sunlight, golden showers, and the asphalt giving off that delicious smell it gets when it's warm and wet. I've always wondered what it is that causes that. But anyway, when I got home, the front door was open, and my mother was nowhere in sight. I went to the kitchen, where I found a BLT – my favorite sandwich – waiting for me on the counter, next to a glass of chocolate milk. Bobby was asleep in the family room, which was sealed off with one of those contraptions that look like little tennis nets. I stepped over it with my milk and my BLT and settled in front of the television to watch some cartoons.

"It was only about fifteen minutes later, during a few seconds of dead air between commercials, that I heard the low rumbling sound coming from the garage. I ventured on out there, switched on the garage light and discovered my mother behind the wheel of our station wagon. Her head was tilted back against the seat, and she looked like she was asleep. I knocked on the door, but she didn't answer. Then I tried all of the door handles, but they were all locked.

"I slid around to the back to check the rear door, and there I found the strangest thing… a black rubber hose taped to the exhaust pipe, and stretching up through a crack at the top of the rear driver's side window. The window opening was taped closed, sealing off the inside of the car.

"Only then did I recognize the set-up from an old movie that my mother and Bobby and I had watched after one of her performances. *So that's what Mom is up to*, I thought. *She's playing another game with us.*

"I went to the porch in front of the kitchen door and sat there watching her, but I thought it was strange that she wasn't singing this time, and she wasn't making those big ballet gestures with her arms. Still, I thought, maybe this time she would die first, and then sing, and then I would laugh at her little joke and clap and yell 'Brava! Brava!' and then we'd go inside and she'd make cookies for us. And I would playfully scold her for trying to trick me like that, for dying first and then singing.

"But I waited another twenty minutes and my mother still didn't move. Not only that, but the fumes had begun to seep out of the car and into the garage, and I was starting to feel nauseous. I went to the big garage door and turned the handle, but could only manage to push it halfway open. The fumes cleared out a little, though, and I could breathe better. I went back to the porch and resumed my waiting.

"A few minutes later the door lifted up the rest of the way, and there was old Mr. Shoriff, with a curious look on his face. He was about to ask me something when he saw my mother in the car, spotted the rubber hose in the exhaust pipe and said a bunch of crackly-sounding words that I'd never heard before. He went to the window and ripped out the hose, then ran around the car, trying all the door handles. I tried to tell him it was okay, that my mother and I were just playing a little game, but he wouldn't listen. Instead he shoved me away, grabbed a baseball bat from the shelf and started smashing all the windows. The glass fell to the floor of the garage in thousands of little diamonds, and smoke curled out from the top of the interior. Mr. Shoriff managed to unlock the passenger-side door and reach over my mother to turn off the ignition, then he held a hand to my mother's neck. He whispered some more of those crackly words and slipped back out the door, standing there with his hands on his knees, gasping for breath and repeating the words, 'Oh my God, Oh my God, Oh my God.' His face was very red, and he was coughing from the smoke.

"It was all a great show for me, of course, all the flying glass and the smoke, and then the flashing lights of the police cars and the fire engines, and all the adults of the neighborhood walking around talking in hushed, excited tones. And I kept waiting for my mom to wake up and start singing, and then the neighbors would laugh and applaud and throw flowers at her feet.

"They took me to my grandma's house, where I was carried upstairs and tucked into bed, even though it was hours before my bedtime. And I stayed up past midnight, anyway, because I heard all those people downstairs, and they were all singing to each other, only it wasn't my mom's kind of singing, and it wasn't my grandma's big butterfly voice – it was my kind of singing, the kind I would make up for my death scenes at school. And I was terribly excited, because I didn't know there were so many people who sang exactly like me."

You can't tell a story like that without working yourself into something of a daze, and once I regained my bearings I realized the sky-blue memory of Indiana had closed back up, the sky had grown dark, and it was raining, bringing up the smell of the grass along the clearing and tapping out hundreds of little beats on the roof of the belvedere.

I turned and found Gabriella kneeling on the grass, frozen in place, the rain turning her hair into wet ropes. Her hand was clenched in a tight fist, and streaks of blackberry juice ran out between her fingers.

I found myself in a clear and calm kind of shock, and was unable to react normally when Gabriella came to me. She put both arms around the statue and kissed his marble brow, then buried her face in his hair and kept crying.

Renata Tebaldi

"I'll go alone and far as the echo from the churchbell. There, amid the white snow; there, amid the clouds of gold – there where the earth appears as but a recollection."
   --*La Wally*

I drive the length of Oregon. The radio slaps me with a four-word sentence. I stop at the Shakespeare festival, trekking the Christmas-lit streets for a latte, rubbing a jigsaw piece between my fingers.

This grieving makes no sense. I don't know you. Everything you've given me is locked away on vinyl and aluminum. My loss is precisely nothing. But once, you took hold of my tangled hearing and untied the knots.

Jenny sits at the kitchen table, her eyes growing wide. You've never heard Tebaldi? She reaches for the stereo: an impossibly broad soprano voice, constructed of butter, an aircraft carrier tracing cadenzas like a speedboat. She tells me you're alive, residing in Italy. This does not seem possible.

I have made no secret of my fixation. My friends will send condolences, as if I have lost a favorite aunt. I will read reports of you at San Marino, breathing your last, one eye on the hills.

On the night of four words, I scale the Siskiyous, strangely energized, the roadsides patching with snow. My head fills with Catalani, Renata loosing her dovish triplets as she climbs the white mountains, untethered.

First published in Terrain.org

"The story *is* the ballet. Otherwise, it would all just be a bunch of steps."

--Karen Gabay, ballerina

Marcello's Lament

Starving baritone finds the stone on a
black sand beach covered in driftwood

(If I said the wood was white as bones
I would be giving it away.)

He kneels on the sand where the
ocean comes through the rocks
and reaches into the ribs of a burnt-out cello
plowing a pyramid of blackened
chars until he fingers the edges of its
mineral heart and
pulls it into the sun.

(If I said it was as red as Betelgeuse
I would be lying.)

The stone is a jealous stone
it takes away his lovers
takes away his sleep
leaves his pockets thin and sallow

She is Musetta
the woman you cannot have
but if you hold her to your ear she will
sing you bright waltzes and
turn her lollipop eyes at you across the café.

But the song and the glance are not enough,
so Marcello takes the stone and grinds it up,
spreads it across his Sunday salad

(If I said the dressing was
Roquefort I would be saying too much.)

The fragments trunkle their way through his
veins and gather at the aorta,
pressing northward to make his heart skip
on nights when Artemis falls awry and
mountainside lanterns burst like
meteors through the Paris streets.

Years after Mimi's last breath
he comes back to the sea to bare his
skin to the inkwell sky and
wait for Orion's belt to burn him down,
leaving a coal as red as Betelgeuse
for the timpani waves to steam away.

First published in Eclectic Literary Forum

"On the singles market, struggling writers rank somewhere below ex-cons, carnival ride operators and male day-care workers."

--Bill Burman, playwright

Is Your Partner a Shadow Writer?

Take this quiz to determine if your beloved is joyful or jealous of your way with words.

First published in Writer's Digest

Perhaps the most potent idea to come out of Julia Cameron's landmark 1992 book, *The Artist's Way*, is the notion of the Shadow Artist, an archetypal figure who tries to compensate for his own blocked creativity by latching onto an actual artist and lavishing praise on her.

Oh, I know. You're thinking, *What's so bad about being lavished with praise?* You might feel differently on that eventual morning when Shnookums rolls over in bed and says, "Honey, it's great that you're an artist and all, but when are you going to get a real job?" Because adoration, left in the sun for too long, has a way of turning to bitter, coagulating resentment – and you have the nerve to be living your partner's dream!

Congratulations – you have just been targeted for a lengthy campaign of passive-aggressive sabotage from a Shadow Writer.

The obvious thing for a writer to do is to avoid these people like the lactose intolerant avoid ice cream. But it ain't easy, because many of them resemble normal, even likable human beings. With that in mind, I offer the following quiz. Find out now: is your partner a shadow writer?

1. When my Hot Potatah goes to a karaoke bar, he likes to...
A. Have a drink and listen to the singers belt out a few songs.
B. Have a couple of drinks and try out one of his favorite songs.
C. Have several drinks and try to get everyone else to sing one of his favorite songs.

2. My Pug-Nose Dream has some killer ideas that she'd like to try out as soon as she...
A. Gets some vacation time.

B.   Takes a writing class.
C.   Gets Stephen King to drop that nasty restraining order.

3. My Bubbelah says that the best thing about being an author would be...
A.   Getting to share his ideas with the public.
B.   Improving his ability to express himself.
C.   Getting to wear tweed whenever he wanted!

4. If my Reason for Being and I were playing Scrabble, and I spelled out "effervescence" over two triple-word scores for a total of 192 points, she would...
A.   Congratulate me on my linguistic skill.
B.   Jokingly stab herself with an invisible knife.
C.   Douse the board with gasoline, light it on fire, and toss it over the balcony into the busy intersection below.

5. When my Studmuffin meets a published author, he likes to...
A.   Ask her about her latest project.
B.   Ask her for advice on writing.
C.   Give her a list of five or six books that she really ought to read.

6. If I decided to leave writing for a more stable career, my Pookie would...
A.   Help me to carefully consider my options before making a decision.
B.   Tell me that whatever I decided was fine by her.
C.   Act elated, then dump me for a poet.

7. My Main Man's favorite device for developing ideas is...
A.   Clustering.
B.   Speedwriting.
C.   Searching "writer" on match.com.

8. On the night of my book release party, my Huggy Bear is likely to ask...
A.   Isn't this exciting?
B.   Are you nervous?
C.   Why is it always about you?

9. When pressed, my Darling Dude would admit that he puts off writing because...
A.   His parents wanted him to be a doctor.
B.   He has a fear of rejection.
C.   Why bother writing when some big asteroid's going to hit the Earth anyway, the only survivors will be cockroaches, and have you ever seen a cockroach trying to use a typewriter? It's pathetic.

10. I knew my Squirrelly Girl was interested in literature when she...
A.   Asked me what I thought of magical realism.
B.   Mentioned a poetry reading she had attended.
C.   Showed up for our first date in a negligee made entirely from typewriter ribbons.

11. When I wake up after an all-night deadline writing session, I know that my Don Juan will...
A.   Make sure there's a pot of coffee on.
B.   Give me a nice neck rub.
C.   Say, "Sure must be nice, getting to sleep in!"

12. If a friend of ours signed a huge publishing contract, my Glamour Goddess would...
A.   Send him a handwritten note of congratulations.
B.   Throw a big party with all of our friends.
C.   Disappear into the night; leave me for him without so much as a typewritter ribbon as a memento.

Scoring: If you answered C on three to four questions, you and your sweetie might need to have a talk. If you answered C on five to seven, you might want to seek counseling. If eight to nine, please send us your sweetie's name and photo so we can put him or her on our Writer's Digest Shadow Writer Hotline. If 10 or more, we hear Mexico is really nice this time of year. (If you answered C on Question 9, read something by William S. Burroughs.)

The Reflector Man

In the novel *Frosted Glass*, Sandy Lowiltry tries to mend her broken heart by checking in to an Indian casino and making mosaics from the beach glass she purloined from her estranged lover. She takes the mosaics to Portland, where she hopes to find some answers from her friend Hessie, owner of the legendary Rimsky-Korsakoffeehouse. When her waitress informs her that Hessie is out of town, Sandy suffers an anxiety attack, and the waitress takes her to a mysterious upstairs room to rest.

What I awoke to I can barely describe. It began with a thunk and clatter, and then the visuals kicked in. I blinked my eyes and made out a wiry hermit with a beard and dark hooded eyes. The walls behind him gave off a rainbow shimmer, crystal cockroaches that squiggled around the room when I moved my head. The hermit scratched his beard and put a hand on either hip.

"Who the fuck are you? Goddammit, I told Hessie to keep this room locked up."

He knelt next to a plastic bag and sorted through its contents, lots of small objects that he clacked around with relish, no doubt enjoying their effect on his drowsy intruder. I raised myself on an elbow.

"Bicycle reflectors."

He gave me an annoyed look. "No shit, Shirley." And went back to his work.

I reached under my quilt to make sure I at least had clothing on, then ran a hand along the wall behind me. The reflectors were lined up seven-deep, triangles, circles, squares, rectangles and ovals in orange, red, green, yellow, blue, even purple, coating the walls in a jungleburst of color. The whole room was done up this way, even the windows and doorjambs, which were trimmed in fire-engine red. The morning sun shot through a side window and lit up a swath of amped-out sparkle, like citric acid made visual.

Hermit-guy sat on his haunches, having sorted out a dozen orange triangles, and took a good long study of me.

"So what's your story, futon-girl? Too many frozen lemon cheesecakes? Triple-mocha heart attack?"

"The Puccini Table."

He let out a rough, squeaky laugh. "Ah-haha! I told them that fucking thing was trouble. Liabilities, man! Lie-uh-bilities."

"So," I said, sweeping a hand at the room. "Is this one of Hessie's preposterous notions?"

"This," he said, "is my preposterous life's work. The canvas, yes, was provided by Madame Nygaard, as was a seriously sweet commission. Hessie is a goddamn artist's wet dream, and although this setting does lack a certain mobility, it will get much more exposure than some fussy millionaire's living room."

I looked at his triangles. "So are those for the orange cross-hatches behind you?"

"Ah, futon-girl has an eye! Yes, although I intend to fade them out along the top, just to be a prick, and then I will weave some snaky yellow ovals to steal away the symmetry."

"That's good," I said.

"Approval is nice," he said. "But it's not what I need. What I need is to not give a flying fuck about what anyone thinks until I'm done, which is why I wanted this room locked up. Nothing worse for clouding the vision than worthless fucking mid-work commentary. Afterward, you can love it, hate it, throw dog shit on it, so long as I've reached the point where there's not a damn thing I can do about it."

"Could I tell you it's one of the most gorgeous things I've ever seen?"

Hermit-guy stood and clapped the dust from his hands. "Now that," he said, "is the kind of generalized ass-kissing that a guy can deal with."

"Oh, it's not ass-kissing. I'm an artist myself."

He delivered a theatrical slap to his forehead and looked to the ceiling. "And she was doing so well. So. How long have you been an artist?"

I was not about to actually speak the words "three weeks," but my expression gave me away.

"How many apartments have you been kicked out of?" he said. "How many credit cards have you run into the ground? How many lovers dumped you after the three-month excitement of dating an artist wore off and she realized you were broke? How many times… have you purchased gas for your car… with the pennies rolled up from your coin jar?"

"I… uh…"

"You get the point, Gladys? You use that word 'artist' around some of my long-suffering friends, and we might have to glaze your white yuppie ass and stick you in a kiln."

"Yuppie?"

"Oh yes. No one ever thinks they're a yuppie. Look at that perfect coiffure, sister. Check out that Sedona sweatshirt. You may as well be wearing a Three Tenors baseball cap, for Chrissake. And I'll bet anything you drive some junior SUV with a CD player and removable seats."

All true, of course. But I would have given anything if he could sense my sincerity, if he could understand the month-long rebirth of my eyeballs. He seemed to reconsider, scuffling a hand through his salt-and-pepper hair.

"Oh, I'm sorry already. I'm just a bitter old artist. Feel free to stick around and watch. Quietly. You like jazz?"

"Sure."

"Okay then! That's a start. Name's Jonathon."

"Sandy," I said.

Jonathon grunted and switched on a tape deck covered with smears of black and gray. Out came Sarah Vaughan, that funny pseudo-British lisp, a swingy version of "I Feel Pretty." I loved watching the track of his thoughts, a little bullet that traveled from eyes to head to hands, then burst forth in matador sweeps as he dabbed a reflector with adhesive and fixed it to a perfect spot. After an hour, I had to let out a question or I would burst.

"So how long?"

"Isn't that kind of personal?"

"How many years," I scolded.

"Twenty-three torturous, impoverished, glo-ree-uss years."

"Any big successes?"

"Every single thing I've ever made. Every time I ignored some flathead who told me I should do something more practical. Including the painters, I might add. They hate this shit."

"Money?"

"Sold a piece in Seattle last week… a ten-foot sunrise of yellow, orange, little flakes of red. Ten thousand dollars."

"Wow!" I exclaimed, a bit too much like a cheerleader.

"And three years ago the Grand Ronde tribes commissioned a bunch of huge-ass geometric things."

"Ohmigod! The Spirit Mountain Casino?"

That was the first thing I had said all morning that seemed to make an impression. He stopped and scratched his beard. "You've been there?"

"Yesterday morning I woke up there. I was sort of… working on my vision."

"Oh, Jesus," he sighed, and turned back to his triangles. "I'm sorry, but you forty-year-old women and this Native American thing…"

Okay, now he was pissing me off.

"Native American craps dice?" I asked. "Native American playing cards?"

"What about them?"

"I use them in mosaics."

He thought about that. "Okay. What else?"

"Frosted glass."

"Sea glass?"

I nodded.

"I love sea glass," he said. "It's so…"

"Random? Organic? Fusion of man and nature?"

"Say! There may be an artist in there after all. Y'got any slides?"

Having passed through such fierce gauntlets, I took this as the highest of compliments. "I've got the actual mosaics," I said. "They're just outside, in my... SUV."

"Oh-hoh!" he roared. "Yuppie girl! Yuppie girl!"

"Yeah, yeah, so I got money. All the more reason for *you* to kiss *my* ass, honey. Let's see..." I counted the points on my fingers. "Loaded yuppie lady, crazy about art, crazy about *your* art, might want to pay ridiculous sums of money for your art..."

"Stop right there!" said Jonathon. He stepped down from his footstool and rubbed his hands on a rag. "What do you say we head outside for some fresh air?"

Jonathon had some blunt critiques – the pastels could have been manipulated more carefully, the six-section piece was much too anal-retentive – but when he got to my craps-dice, his eyes lit up. "If you'd really like to be an artist," he said, "you can start right here. Such sly humor!"

We were both feeling like some exercise, so I took him to my raisable section of drawbridge, where we watched the Willamette's glacier-like course. Jonathon evidently had a thing for bridges, because he gave me a pretty impressive rundown: Hawthorne Bridge, built in 1910, one of the oldest lift bridges in the world, both feared and beloved by the locals for its rickety steel-mesh roadways. I was almost disappointed when he brought up his wife, a painter who created real-life scenes populated with primitive, cartoon-like figures. She took the narratives from a childhood of incest and molestation.

"When I first saw her works, I was in such a state of awe – the sheer bluntness, the incredible courage it took to portray such ugliness. It made me feel like my own work was too... I don't know, decorative, socially irrelevant. But then I took her to my studio, and she loved it! She said she was amazed by its imagination and humor – in fact, she saw in my work what was perhaps lacking in her own. Our personalities fit into a surprisingly common pattern: the intense artist who's incredibly easy-going, the humorous artist who can be a real prick... as you found out this morning."

He fell silent for a moment, lost in the river. I played a little game, testing my vision.

"I love the water here," I said. "It reminds me of..."

"Green marble?" he said.

"Exactly." I wrapped my hands around the railing, smooth and cool in my grip. "So do you and Marta have any kids?"

"No. Marta wanted to cut the string. Not that she was concerned about herself – she's the gentlest person on the planet – but the very act of child-bearing would bring back too many shadows. It also gave her a chance to pull the drain on a very toxic gene pool. She was their last chance."

"Do you ever feel like you're missing out on something?"

He edged up to my shoulder. "There are a lot of things I'm not doing. I'm not climbing Mount Everest, I'm not swimming with dolphins in the Virgin Islands, and I'm not playing mid-striker for the Argentinean World Cup soccer team. If you think too much about the things you're missing, you're apt to miss out on the things you're not missing. Look at that room I'm working on. I'm getting good solid American currency to revel in color and light on a daily basis.

"No." he continued. "Rather than giving the earth more children it doesn't need, I will leave behind lovely radiant works of art. That room at Rimsky's? His name is going to be Jerry. He's a terrific little kid... and once I'm gone, he'll have all kinds of friends who come to visit and ooh and ahh at the very sight of him. Are you all right?"

I couldn't help myself. That same slice of sun was knifing over Portland to sow Jonathon's beard with a ring of sparks. I reached out to gather them in.

"Who are you, Jonathon, who do you work for, and how is it that you know all the answers without knowing the questions?"

Jonathon broke up his beard with a toothy grin. "I'm nothing all that much," he said. "I'm just the reflector man."

"As opera singers who are trained to have excellent diction, we spit a lot on stage while emoting or attempting to get out those consonants. It's an interesting thing to have gotten used to my colleagues spitting on me."

--Betany Coffland, opera singer

The Daffy Duck Syndrome

In the novel *Operaville*, blogger Mickey Siskel finds himself in a budding friendship with his idol, the international diva Maddalena Hart. He's doubly surprised when Maddalena, suffering from some mysterious malady, asks if she can stay the night at his cabin in the Santa Cruz Mountains.

Next to me, something is moving. I squint at the ceiling, pull my arms under me and roll over. It's Maddie, in striped yellow pajamas.

"Mickey? Are you awake? Are you conscious?"

I'm *self*-conscious. Because I tend to sleep in the nude. But I notice that she's lying on top of my comforter, so we still have one degree of separation. A whisper of light seeps through the windows. I'm guessing it's six, six-thirty.

"Um… Hi."

"Hi." She's wide awake, full of energy. "I owe you an explanation. But I can't tell you unless you're fully conscious." She taps a fingernail against her teeth, perhaps the habit of a reformed chewer.

I rub my eyes, throw out my arms and stretch everything else, gaining an immediate preview of all the aches that will follow me for the rest of the day. I manage to generate one-half of a smile.

"Shoot."

"It's those goddamn minor characters. I'm rushing through costume changes, making my way to the stage, running parts through my head, and I pass the green room, where I see Monsieur Triquet and Olga and they're playing cards with the techies and laughing, and I'm thinking, Why do I have all this *freaking* stage time? This is crazy! Why am I doing this impossible thing? I have placed myself in a position where the Sunday afternoons of thousands of people, the day's wages of a couple hundred musicians, ushers, administrators, et cetera and a notable percentage of the local economy depends on my doing this horribly difficult thing. Stepping onto that stage is like a bungee-jumper stepping off the platform. Every instinct of self-preservation tells you that you are putting your trust in a thin elastic band – your training, your memorization, your rehearsals, your stage skills – to prevent you from becoming a messy smudge on the rocks below. But I do it. I take that leap and these sounds fly from my mouth and I fill the artificial soul and emotions of this fictional character. And I do understand that I'm very good at what I do, but sometimes I don't really understand *how* I do what I do. What I'm afraid of is…"

An idea lands on her satellite dish, her eyes widen. She grips my shoulder.

"When I was a kid, I would watch these cartoons where the character, let's say Daffy Duck, would be thrust out over the edge of the cliff. But he wasn't *aware* of it, so he would just hover in mid-air. However, the second he looked down and *realized* where he was – *that's* when he would fall. (Of course, part of the joke was that Daffy kept forgetting that he was a duck, and could fly.) But here's the lesson: it's not the gravity that makes you fall, it's the *realization* of gravity.

"On Sunday, during the final act, for the briefest of moments, I realized that I didn't know my next line, and for just a moment I froze. Jesus, bless him, saw my predicament and bought me a second by kissing my hand. Then the conductor, Donald, slowed the tempo just a bit – a grain of sand, but just enough for me to recall the next line and smuggle it into the flow of the music. I'm sure that no one in the audience knew a thing. But for me, for just that one lightning-flash, a chink opened up in my little world, and through that chink I glimpsed the enormous void of gravity and impossibility that underlies everything I do. It scared the hell out of me."

I fully expect her to break into tears, but this is not a crying thing, it's something closer to the brain. Anxiety. Fear. She tucks her head into my shoulder, I wrap an arm around her as best a civilized-but-naked man can, and I stroke her hair. I am Mickey, who solves all problems by stroking hair. We lie in pools of faint light for fifteen minutes. Maddie's breathing slows to a regular pace and she says, "Mickey? Could you make me some breakfast?"

Postmark

Salieri tut-tutting Mozart at the
volleyball match and the apartments so
regally named: Duxbury, Cambridge, Wilsonion.

Armed with a ballcap, scouring the
treetops for bald eagles make this special make this
deeper than a looped-over cowpath to the
library the coffeehouse the bookstore the
café the biblioteque the roasting company like a
volleyball match like a bald eagle at a
piano pecking out *Figaro*, string over
string in a chickenwire weave, mixing up the
streets to cheat the demon backtrack:

Tacoma Yakima Ruston McCarver the
boxcar line the salmon fry the raccoon
wood and the bald eagles hanging in the
air like volleyballs.

I roost at the Windsor regally
named and scour the mailbox for bald eagles.
Salieri was no slouch.

First published in Terrain.org

The Perfect Latte

Andre plays classical guitar at the How You Bean, a coffeehouse in Boulder, Colorado. He plays for tips, but really he plays for Roxanne, who works behind the counter.

Andre is drawn to a well-defined type, olive-skinned girls with robust features and dark eyes. He spent his high school years with Maria Frenghetti, an exuberant Catholic beauty who chose graduation day to sacrifice their love on the pyres of religion and family.

His first night at the Bean, Roxanne barely registers. She is slim, red-haired, freckled, a quick entry to his Not-My-Type file (he does not do this consciously, but his filters are ruthlessly consistent). He plays for two hours, to meager applause but several smiles, plus sixteen dollars in his guitar case.

"Say, Andre?" It's the tall, red-haired barista. "Did you want your drink? You get a free drink."

"Oh. Sure. How 'bout a double latte? I'll pick it up after this last song."

He plays an arrangement of "Purple Haze" by Jimi Hendrix. It's a remarkable rendition, done in the baroque style. You have to really pay attention to catch the tune. Andre savors the raised eyebrows and chuckles of recognition. An aging hippie yells, "Rock on!" Five more dollars migrate to his case.

"That was great!" says the barista. "I'll leave your drink on the table."

"Thanks." He gathers his tips, lowers his guitar into the case, then turns to find a work of art.

It sits in a tall, narrow glass, like a clear two-inch pipe with a handle. The bottom layer is four inches of steamed milk, the middle an inch-wide strip of espresso the color of charred wood. The top is two inches of milk foam, edging past the brim, one feathered dollop flipped over like a pompadour.

Only once has Andre seen such a thing – a caffe in Florence, on a tour of Italy after his first year of college. A woman who could be Maria Frenghetti's mother laughs when he sips at the foam.

"No!" she says. "Presto!"

He's not good with Italian, but he does know musical notion. "Presto" means "quickly." So he swallows. The espresso bites into his tongue, then slips away in a wash of hot milk and foam. It's like rough sex. In his mouth. He has trouble expressing to his friends.

He has more trouble explaining this to the baristas of America, where efficiency has buried all other considerations. He refers to it by one filthy word: sploosh. Everything dumped in at once, a warmish, beige beverage. He tries to explain the Italian method with adjectives: "parfait," "striped," "separated." He turns to ad-hoc lessons: *Now pour the espresso down the back of the spoon, so it goes through the foam, but not into the milk.*

But life gets busy, and you shouldn't have to give five minutes of instructions every time you want a latte. So he gives way to the sploosh majority, and he drinks from cardboard cups.

But now – this. He studies the perfect striations of brown and white, then tips the glass and drinks. *Presto.*

Andre plays again the following week, and he finds himself slipping up, on a piece he has played since he was six. These are small flaws: releasing a chord too early, dropping a note from an arpeggio. Nothing that an average listener would notice. But it bothers him. He understands that perfection is not, logically speaking, attainable. But if you're not going to at least chase it, what's the purpose?

He knows what it is. Too many of his focal points are occupied by the image of Roxanne's latte. He takes an early break and requests his free drink.

"Double latte?" she asks.

"Exactly the same."

"Ah." She smiles. "A connoisseur." She packs the grounds into a disc and slides it into a machine. Andre stands at the counter, watching.

"So what do you call it? Parfait? Striped?"

Roxanne twitches her lips in thought. "Pretty-style."

"Pretty-style."

She laughs. "I know. Corny. But it's the only expression everyone seems to understand."

She pours the milk, then lays in the foam, till it comes to an inch from the top. Then she brings the shot cup to the edge of the glass.

"No!" says Andre. "You pour it freehand? No spoon?"

Roxanne keeps her eye on the brown trickle. "All that is required... is the touch... of a neurosurgeon."

A dark line appears between milk and foam and rises to a solid band, as if someone has painted it on the glass. She covers her pour spot with a cap of foam, then stands back to admire her work.

"You are a goddess of the caffeine arts," says Andre.

That night he crosses his front lawn, huffing steam into the cold air. He pauses and sets down his guitar case. A full moon is filtering the madrone, silvering its smooth limbs. Andre sees Roxanne's shoulders, bare and slender, turning away as the espresso bites into his tongue.

Roxanne realizes that her job is predominantly customer-service. She also knows that her age and appearance fall into a certain type: tall, high-cheekboned, girl-next-door (Julia Roberts comes up). She is a magnet for heartbroken forty-year-olds.

But most of them want just a conversation, a smile. Just the fact that she remembers their names and favorite drinks brightens their faces. She is careful to draw boundaries, but time is her friend – always another customer, another chore to keep the encounter brief. And they all understand.

She is protective of her true affections – rarely gives them out – and is very clear on the type of man who buzzes her circuits. He is big, a barrel-chested guy who could squeeze her to a pulp. Not that she wants that, but just the idea of all that suppressed force. In the old high-school fantasy game, her picks would be Russell Crowe, a young Sean Connery, Brando in *Streetcar*.

Slight, effeminate Andre doesn't stand a chance – until he starts playing. The deftness of his fingering captivates her. His choice of material – piano transcriptions from Poulenc and Satie – has her lifting in her shoes to listen. He also knows a good musical joke, dropping a quote from "Hotel California" into a Granados tango. She's the only one who notices.

There's a reason for this. Roxanne is a piano student. Her teachers love her playing, and encourage her to give recitals. But her ears tell her differently. She knows that perfection is a ruthless master, but she wants to be at least somewhere in the same county before she exposes herself to an audience. She tells no one about her studies – not even her closest friends – and when she hears someone like Andre, her feelings are confirmed.

The thing with the lattes catches her off-guard. She never realized they were so exceptional – but then, she's never had such a knowledgeable audience. It reminds her of a trip she took to Italy, where espresso is almost a religion. And it gives her hope. If her hands are really so adept, perhaps someday they will pour a perfect Rachmaninoff.

Still, these feelings are self-centered and intellectual – not the same as attraction. Perhaps Andre's lack of manliness is the price for his brilliant sensitivity.

They are working a bright, cold Sunday when Roxanne feels a sound at her shoulder, like a rustling newspaper. When she turns, a dark blur flings itself at her head. She ducks and lets out a girly shriek. The blur zips across the room and strikes the window with a *thwack!*

Oh God, she thinks. It's a bird. With lots of door traffic and lots of crumbs, this happens at least once a month, but she never gets used to it. The customers panic; the bird panics. The plate glass affords a deadly illusion.

The first impact renders this one semi-conscious. He settles on a windowsill, a dark brown sparrow blinking his eyes like a boxer on the mat. The customers buzz and chatter.

The music stops. Andre paces across the room, holding his sportcoat like a shield. He brings it to the sill, trapping the sparrow underneath, then bunches the sides into a sack. He carries his package outside, wingflaps ticking the fabric, then settles his coat to the ground and whips it away like a magician's cape. The bird shoots off for the nearest tree.

Andre watches him go, then re-enters to applause and whistles. He returns to his chair and says, "For my next trick, I will play the guitar!"

Roxanne feels a pleasant tingle running the roof of her mouth.

Roxanne's best friend is I-Chun, a Taiwanese tomboy who wears thin rectangular spectacles, several piercings and a white skunk-stripe through her jet-black hair. When she smells a clove cigarette, she knows that Roxanne is troubled, and retreats to the back alley to find out why.

"'Zup, girlfriend?" She slides down the wall to sit next to her on the sidewalk.

Roxanne takes a long drag. The sharp spice numbs the end of her tongue.

"Guy."

"'Nother strappin' lothario?"

"Nah. Guitarist."

"That guy from NedRed? I didn't think you went for longhairs."

"Classical guitarist."

I-Chun bugs out her eyes in that way she knows she's good at.

"Geez!" says Roxanne. "No need to go all Academy Awards on me."

"You're going a bit far afield, Roxy. But – what's the problem?"

Roxanne squints her eyes and takes another drag. "Goddamn lattes. All he ever talks about."

"Well, you are the Queen of La…"

"Stop right there!" Roxanne waves a threatening finger. "There is more to yours truly than a… beverage. I am a luscious piece of feminine flash, and I am about ready to hear that from someone besides myself."

"You are a luscious piece of feminine flesh."

"And the second I go lezzie, you're at the top of my list. But back to my point."

"Do you have anything else in common?"

Roxanne hesitates. Is it time to tell I-Chun about pianos? "No," she says. "Not a thing."

I-Chun takes the cigarette and steals a puff. "I got it," she says. "Change the pattern of discourse. Fuck one up."

"Fuck up a… latte?"

I-Chun pantomimes a witch throwing two toads into a pot. "Sploosh! Give him the world's doggiest latte."

"Oh not sploosh! Wouldn't I be breaking some ethical code?"

"The hell with ethics! This is sex."

"Or romance."

"Yeah. Right."

Andre places the glass on the counter like the opening exhibit in a homicide case. Roxanne stops, mid-cappuccino, and pretends to look puzzled.

"Hi. What's up?"

"Excuse the language, Roxanne, but what… is that?"

"What language?"

"Fill in the blanks."

Roxanne shouts "Double cap!" to the coffeehouse, then returns to Andre. "Sorry. I was in a hurry. I can make another, if you like."

"Well, yes! Geez, Roxanne, I didn't think you were even capable of something like this."

"Is that the only reason you like me?" She tries to make it a joke, but comes up short.

Andre thinks about it. "If I played really crappy, strummy guitar, would you still like me?"

"Yes!"

"But would you think less of me?"

She sighs, defeated. "Yes. Because your playing is lovely."

"There! It's no crime for me to appreciate the care and skill you put into your work."

All this logic is pissing her off. And there's a customer at the register. Does he have no psychic powers at all? Does she really have to put this into words?

"Name one other thing you like about me. You have five seconds."

He leans into the counter. "You have the most elegant shoulders I have ever seen."

Andre sits in his basement apartment, watching television. That's it. I have killed off a perfectly good gig. Why couldn't I say she had a nice smile? Good breath? A cute nose?

Roxanne sits at her dining room table. She spies her reflection in the window. She turns her chair till she's facing away, then looks back over her shoulder. *Elegant.*

Andre is cordial, friendly, but no closer. He natters on about lattes as if he has been banned from talking about anything else.

"A spell," says I-Chun.

Roxanne raises her eyebrows in that way she knows she's good at. "You *are* kidding."

I-Chun throws her hands up. "I've got nothin' to work with. Why don't you just ask him out?"

"No. I need him to ask me out."

"Jesus! Hope a bus into the twenty-first century."

"It's not about that. It's because I have no idea if he's really interested. Oh, God. Do you suppose he's gay?"

"Hah! You supermodels are all alike. 'If he doesn't like me, he's *got* to be gay.' A spell, sister. That's my last word."

I-Chun heads back inside as Roxanne complains after her: "But I don't know any spells!"

Two hours later, it's time for Andre's break. Roxanne fills the disc with espresso and looks around. Cardamom – the spice they use for Turkish coffee. She shakes it into the grounds and locks the disc into the machine. Under the hiss, she leans close to the shot cup and whispers, "Courage."

She is stacking chairs on tables when Andre stops by, guitar case in hand.

"Was there something… different tonight?"

"Sure. I added some cardamom."

"I like it."

"Good."

A silence drifts in like a tule fog. Lots of room for someone to ask someone out on a date. Maybe they could meet for a cup of coffee.

"Well," he says. "Gotta go!"

"Goodnight," says Roxanne. She lifts another chair.

Andrea sits on his couch, working through a new Scarlatti. It's getting worse! That look on her face. She's so popular. It seems like half the town knows her. What'm I doing even thinking about it? Oh Jesus, Andre – read the fucking music.

Roxanne continues the cardamom, to no discernible effect. If anything, Andre seems more distant – even vaguely annoyed. Then he's gone, replaced by a guy named Martin. Roxanne stops by on his break.

"Do you know Andre?"

"Sure," says Martin. "He's in my composition class. He sort of passed this gig on to me."

"Did he say why?"

"Heavy class load, somethin' like that."

"Okay. Thanks."

"Hey, thanks for the latte. It was screamin'."

"Yeah. No problem."

The next three months are winter. The short days and foul weather conspire to drive Roxanne into the ground. Even the snow, which used to excite her. Now it reminds her of lost chances, the dying earth – some connection she has failed to make. She spends hours in the rehearsal room, playing Schubert sonatas and Chopin nocturnes, forcing the sad music into her veins so she can bleed it back out.

On the first day of March, she sits in a corner with her biology textbook. A shadow comes over her table. It's Andre.

"Andre! Where've you… It's good to see you."

"It's good to see you. I've been kinda… busy. But today's been really rough, and I thought, What you really need is one of Roxanne's perfect lattes. But I guess… you're not on?"

"No. But I'll make you one. Be right back."

Roxanne sprinkles cardamom into the disc, whispers "Courage," then stands there, staring into the cup.

What the hell am I doing?

She fills a glass with ice and pours in the espresso, then drinks it down at a shot. Shards of light bulbs tinkle into her brain stem. Then she makes a perfect latte.

"Here ya go, sailor."

"Ah, perfection!" says Andre. "Thanks. I will leave you to your studies."

"No," says Roxanne. "There's a price for this service. You will sit here while I pick your brain."

Andre smiles and joins her. "Sure. Whatcha got?"

"Well first – that transcription from Ravel. Where did you find that? You see, I'm studying piano, and I…"

Roxanne plays classical piano at the How You Bean, a coffeehouse in Boulder, Colorado. She plays for tips, but really she plays for Andre, who sits across the room and watches her elegant shoulders.

"Language is a way to help our vision of the world match up to its reality."

--Dorianne Laux, poet

Vice-Versa

Can you have it both ways? Here, three author/poets discuss why prose writers should try poetry, and why poets should pen prose.

First published in Writer's Digest

As a career author/poet, I am frequently the only novelist at the poetry reading, the only poet at the fiction workshop. I find this puzzling, because the two disciplines are so wonderfully complementary.

I suspect that this separation of forms derives from an ancient and powerful prejudice. Poetry is such a unique art that someone invented the word "prose" to mean, very specifically, "not-poetry" (in the same way that "gentile" means "not Jewish"). I think authors envision poets conjuring their weirdly shaped stanzas in witches' cauldrons, while poets imagine authors chained to enormous boulders of narrative, inching them painfully forward.

Well, nonsense. Poetry and prose are both expressions of written language, inextricably attached to that thing we do when we open our mouths and sound comes out. And there are vast benefits to be culled from the territories in which they overlap.

But don't take my word for it. Take the words of Diane Ackerman, Kim Addonizio and Naomi Shihab Nye, three of today's most successful author/poets, who agreed to help us explore the advantages of being a "double threat."

How would you compare the creative processes of prose and poetry?

Ackerman: Among the many kinds of nests writers create for the feathered mysteries that live inside them, I find poems more like an arrangement of nesting stones, and prose more like woven mud-and-twig nests. The architecture of each is slightly different, and has its own rules, but both are good places to hatch ideas.

Nye: I would say they are very close friends, next-door neighbors, a teaspoon of almond extract here, a snip of fresh mint leaves there. They feed one another. They sit down together. There is no clash. They never argue. I rarely "turn one into the other," however. A poem starts out as a poem, a prose as prose. It's an instinct, I think. Good friends know when it's their turn to talk.

Addonizio: The image that just came to mind is this: the bottom-feeding fish have swum up and started leaping out of the water as thoughts, ideas, bits of language. I can tell the poem-fish from the prose-fish; the poem leaps higher, and its arc can be seen all at once, which is the great pleasure of writing a poem. In prose – especially when working on a novel – everything feels more furtive, less obvious. You can grab the poem-fish barehanded, but the novel requires sitting for a long time with your lure floating on the surface of the water.

How do the two forms interact? Do you ever borrow phrases or ideas from one to use in the other?

Ackerman: When I was an undergraduate, I had two female cats that got pregnant at the same time (my roommate let in a tom one night), and they had their kittens within days of each other. I guess their scents got confused, because they began stealing and nursing each other's kittens. My prose and poetry sometimes steal each other's kittens, as I try to decide where an image or observation belongs.

Addonizio: Once in a while I've found myself stealing a phrase from one of my poems and slipping it into a novel. I know it's wrong, but I just can't help myself. It's like spiking the punch.

Does one form ever bring up a subject that you end up pursuing with the other form?

Addonizio: When I wrote my second book of poems, *Jimmy & Rita*, I did it as a verse novel. It's a story you have to read straight through, from first poem to last. I never considered writing it as a novel, maybe because I was too terrified to try the novel form. But later, I continued the story of those two characters – as a novel. I wanted to find out what happened to them after *Jimmy & Rita* ended. And this time, it felt like it could only be explored in prose, with a deeper attention to the lives and circumstances of the characters.

Ackerman: There are times when, after writing a nature essay, I find I have lots of emotional spill-over and want to work on some poems. *Jaguar of Sweet Laughter*, for example, includes many poems set in the Amazon and Antarctic, which I wrote while traveling there to write essays I included in *The Moon by Whale Light*. And sensory observations from both trips went into *A Natural History of the Senses*.

Are there are times when you're, in fact, combining the forms? Or at least, writing something in-between?

Ackerman: If I had a choice, every page of my prose books would be intense, image-laden poetry. But I know the sun can't always be at noon in a 300-page book. Books have to have transitions, contrasts, changes of pace. Still, it's the more poetic passages that satisfy me the most. Poetry is a special way of knowing the world, but so is lyrical, imagistic prose; both usher me into a cyclone of intense alertness, in which every sensation and detail leaps out, a kind of deep-play rapture I love.

Addonizio: When we say of something that it is "pure poetry," what we mean is that there is a certain state of being that we connect with through whatever form of art is before us. Because verse on the page has the greatest capacity to bring us to that state through language, we've named it "poetry." So when you take the techniques of verse – lyricism, imagery, and of course concision, metaphor, a heightened rhythmic sense – and use them in prose, the effect is ravishing.

Does the poetic demand for economy of language help you in your prose?

Nye: While working on my (most recent) novel, *Going Going*, I dramatically overwrote about five full drafts. One day I woke up realizing I could cut off the first *eighty pages* and the thing would really fly. So that's what I did…. I thought about how being a poet –

slashing whole stanzas, feeling comfortable identifying the "scaffolding" in a poem and taking it off once the "real poem heart" emerges – helped me do something so dramatic.

Addonzio: Poetry taught me that I must use, as Coleridge put it, "the best words in the best order." I learned to work very hard at revision, to ruthlessly jettison what wasn't working, and to keep challenging myself. I learned, on the practical level, how to be clear and concise, and how to wake up my language. When I turned to fiction, I found that these things were an enormous advantage.

Does the twofold pursuit offer career advantages?

Nye: Prose-writers are paid more than poets. It is a shock to many poets to receive a check for $300 or $400 for a single item (story, essay) – I know it was to me! Poets are used to being paid a copy of the issue and $14.

Addonizio: It was very gratifying to be paid for my first novel, *Little Beauties*. My agent sold the book just before I turned fifty. My first book of poetry came out when I was forty. So I spent many years – before and after publication – working at various jobs and struggling financially. Now I feel I can breathe a bit easier.

What about marketing considerations?

Nye: When my collection of nonfiction personal essays, *Never in a Hurry*, was published, quite a few of my neighbors acted as if I were finally a *real writer*. I had finally published something they felt really comfortable with and actually *read* and recommended to one another! I also like being able to give readings which include both poetry and excerpts from prose – it's easier on the listener sometimes, to have a longer narrative block included.

Addonizio: I have found that readers of my poems – those who have written me to tell me that my work moved them, or mattered to them in some deep way – are amazing people. Poetry has to be sought out, in our culture; it isn't generally put in front of us. Being a poet who is also a novelist means that maybe I can move poetry a bit more into the mainstream – whether it's my own or someone else's.

Does it help to open up the perceptive faculties? And give you new challenges?

Addonizio: I failed miserably as a fiction writer, over and over. I abandoned fiction many times, but something kept drawing me back, until I finally managed to gain some skills. Trying a new form, or simply trying any form of writing, is a difficult but worthwhile lesson. You have to confront your fears and your ego. You don't get past them, but you do grow. Then, of course, insanely, you want to do it all over again.

Ackerman: Writing has always been my form of celebration and prayer, but it's also the way I enquire about the world. Throughout my teens and twenties, poetry was all I knew. I loved trying to reduce something – the way someone walks, the flutter of a monk seal's eyelashes – to the rigorous pungency of an epigram, and still do. But I sometimes craved more elbow room. So I struggled to learn to write prose, which didn't come naturally to me, and was a nightmare chore for years. How I remember putting one sentence at the top of a page, one sentence at the bottom, and having absolutely no idea what to put between them! I worked brutally hard at it for about ten years. Then something finally clicked, and prose became a familiar country. I discovered that, for me at least, writing poetry and prose is like riding a bicycle and a horse – they're different experiences, but many of the same motor skills apply. Now I find it fun, fascinating, sometimes even thrilling to write prose. And my muse is happily miscellaneous. I feel lucky to have been able to use prose as a passport to some of the most astonishing landscapes.

Diane Ackerman is best known for her non-fiction books on science and nature, notably the 1990 best-seller *A Natural History of the Senses*. She has several books of poems, most recently *Origami Bridges: Poems of Psychoanalysis and Fire* (HarperCollins). Her most recent prose book is *An Alchemy of Mind* (Scribner), an exploration of the brain based on the latest neuroscience. She has won many prizes and awards, including a Guggenheim Fellowship, and has the rare distinction of having a molecule named after her: dianeackerone.

Kim Addonizio's debut novel, *Little Beauties*, was released by Simon & Schuster in August 2005. She is the author of four critically acclaimed poetry collections, most recently *What Is This Thing Called Love* (W.W. Norton). Her third collection, *Tell Me* (BOA Editions) was a National Book Award finalist. She also published a book of stories, *In the Box Called Pleasure*, and, with Dorianne Laux, *The Poet's Companion: A Guide to the Pleasures of Writing Poetry*. Addonizio's awards include a Guggenheim Fellowship and two fellowships from the National Endowment for the Arts.

Naomi Shihab Nye is an acclaimed poet, poetry anthologist and young adult novelist. Her collection *19 Varieties of Gazelle: Poems of the Middle East,* was nominated for a National Book Award. Her young adult novel *Habibi* was recently adapted into a stage play. Her latest book of poems, *A Maze Me: Poems for Girls*, and her young adult novel *Going Going* were released earlier this year by Greenwillow/HarperCollins. Nye was born to a Palestinian father and American mother, and grew up in St. Louis, Jerusalem and San Antonio – a diversity of place and heritage that has deeply influenced her writing.

Being Francis

On a Mexican cruise with a legends show – passengers lifted to
godhood. My rivals at the audition opt for white tuxedos and cartoon
impressions, but the crowd is buying none of it. I've been swingin'
all night, and I know you, Francis. I know the lesser titles that light
up the eyes of octogenarians: *French Foreign Legion, Polka Dots
and Moonbeams, There But For You Go I.* I have drunk the milky
swoop of *Witchcraft* sustenatos, the roguish, citified bark, the way
you dare the orchestra on as you contemplate an entrance, the
baritone elixir that makes opera singers weep. The rest is a roll of the
natal dice: vocal cords that bear a passing resemblance, blue eyes,
rhythm in the blood.

I report for the holy relics: the short-brimmed hat, the tux with the
dangling bowtie, the understanding that *My Way* is not a song but a
conversation with a thousand close friends, and make my entrance to
a dark stage, an empty stool, a single spotlight. Pardon me if I have
made use of you, if the citizens of this floating colony embrace me
for tearing off a thread of your gigantic soul.

As the ship slumbers I report to a bar, order the requisite martini and begins this note of thanks. But a man is sitting at the corner like *One For My Baby*, eyeing a Cuban that he told his wife he wouldn't smoke. When faux Frank appears at his side, he hands it over, thanks me for the tune and heads upstairs for his just reward, leaving me to light up and write of love, and jazz, the tang of a gin-soaked olive, the joyous curve of a swinging note, as the hours grow small and the dark Pacific reels past my window.

Stage Blues

In the novel *Outro*, Ruby Cohen gives up on a once-promising Broadway career to move to the Northwest and take care of her troubled brother. She takes her singing to the Karz Bar karaoke lounge in Gig Harbor Washington, where she befriends the hostess, Channy, and hooks up with one of the regulars, Harry. When she and Harry return from a Mexican cruise, she meets Channy for coffee and relates a remarkable story.

Ruby

Everything on the ship had an artistic theme, and the karaoke took place in the Starry Night Lounge, before an enormous wallpaper re-creation of its title work. As you might have guessed, Harry and I went there every night. He had the chance to sic his well-drilled repertoire on a whole new crowd of swooning females, and I had the chance to explore an impressive selection of standards and showtunes. I developed an immediate following among the seniors, who enjoyed swinging and fox-trotting to my songs.

At the end of our first evening, our Australian hostess Lani asked me if I was going to try out for the Legends concert. For the next four evenings, passengers would come to the Starry Night and sing a song by a legendary performer. If the audience decided you were the best at that song, you would appear as that performer in a Vegas-style show before 1,500 of your fellow passengers.

I actually thought of opting out. The contest was obviously aimed at amateurs, and it wouldn't be entirely fair for me to participate. That thought lasted about half a second. If my ship was gonna have a show, *I* was gonna be in it.

One problem: none of the female roles were from jazz or Broadway. I halfway thought of cross-dressing as Sinatra, but I chickened out. So began my journey through the popular music of the late 20th century.

The first night was Aretha, and the song was "Respect." I assumed it was about the singing, and I thought I pretty much nailed it. But then, out comes this perky young Filipina, and she's got *choreography*, for God's sake. So much choreography, in fact, that she's dropping notes right and left. No one seems to notice, and I'm out.

The next night is Madonna, "Like A Virgin." I grew up on that song – hell, I think I lost my virginity to that song. But I've learned my lesson, so I throw in a couple of sexy moves when I can. *However.* The next contestant is this sexy Italian kindergarten teacher from Long Island, and she throws in the kind of moves that *no* kindergarten teacher should *ever* know. At one point, she pulls out a classic Madonna maneuver, lying with her back on the stage while she's singing. So! Am I going to get the part? No way.

My third chance is Gloria Estefan, "The Rhythm is Gonna Get You." I can *totally* pull off Gloria – I grew up in Florida, after all – and I prep myself with some salsa and rhumba moves before adjourning to the Starry Night. But *then…*

The rowdiest pack on the ship is this alumni group from Indiana University. They're easy to spot, because they all wear red, all the time – massing down the fiesta deck, crowding the blackjack tables, doing the frug in the Warhol Club. In the swimming pools, they wear red bathing suits. Nice people, but loud, and the constant red-ness gives off an unsettling Nazi vibe.

I sing a couple of tropical warmups – "Jamaican Farewell," "Girl from Ipanema" – but at nine, when the contest begins, there's a rumbling like someone just lifted the gate at Pamplona. The wide front doors swing open and in rolls the Red Sea, filling every available nook. As you might expect, they're here for a cause: a 50-year-old with dried-out smoker's skin and frizzy hair with traces of several different red dye jobs. She actually seems quite nice, and she throws in some decent Cuban dance moves, but her voice is a creaky, smoked-out mess. Doesn't matter. When the Red Sea explodes, she's a winner.

I can't be the good loser this time. I wait till the next singer takes the mic, then give Harry's hand a squeeze and we make for the back exit. We're halfway through the Internet café when a door opens, and out pops our KJ.

"Lani! How'd you…?"

"Every ship's got its secret passageways," she says. "Look. *That* sort of shit" – she nods back toward the club – "is a truly unfortunate part of my job. It happens at least once a cruise. But I want you to know, I know exactly how good you are, and I know this stuff is *all* beneath your talent, but I can't stand the thought of you not being in that show, and I *really* want you to come back tomorrow night."

"I'm… thanks, Lani. But I don't even know the song."

She hands me a rectangular object wrapped in wires. It's an IPod. "You will, if you listen to that. We usually only give these to the winners, so they can practice for the show. But screw the rules! We're in international waters, right?"

"Oh Lani, I…"

"Oh Lani nothing! Do your homework, young lady. Whoops! Song's over. Bye."

She's back through the door and I'm left floating in flattery. We retreat to the arcade, where Harry and I work out our frustrations on a combination jukebox/electronic drum set (mostly Led Zeppelin) then on to the Matisse jazz lounge for martinis. When we get back to our cabin, I find a mysterious package on my bed. It's a DVD of the Legends concert from a previous cruise. Somebody *really* wants me to get this part.

Which is Britney Spears – "Hit Me Baby One More Time." I never liked it much, but the next morning, when I strapped on the IPod and tried it out, I was surprised to find out how well it suited me. Britney has this deep, low pocket that she slides into, and it seemed to wrap around my voice like a form-fitting dress. After it scratched a few grooves into my synapses, I tried out the DVD and studied the moves of the ship's dancers. (I ignored their Britney, who was Aunt-Zelda-sings-at-your-wedding awful.) If I could work a little of the choreography into my audition, it would give me a nice edge. I pushed our bed to the cabin wall and put myself through some paces. It was pretty sexy stuff; I caught Harry peeking from the bathroom as he shaved.

The costume was a cinch. I picked out a short pleated skirt (intended for some imaginary night of dancing), shiny black shoes that might pass for patent leather, and white knee-high stockings. Then I stole Harry's white dress shirt and tied it above my bare midriff. Voila! The classic parochial slut, and we were off to the bar.

Little do I know, I have become a cause celebre. The regulars are pretty cheesed off about the Red Sea incident, and impressed that I am now risking four-time loserdom. A group of Japanese tourists has migrated to the front row for the sole purpose of cheering me on. I am the 1980 U.S. hockey team, the 1969 Jets. When I begin with Peggy Lee's "Fever" (designed to work up my "sexy"), the crowd lets out a practice uproar.

Come audition time, I'm up first, and I guess I'm better than I expected. I have wisely inserted my dance moves into the generous spaces between the vocal lines, so I can concentrate on one task at a time. Rolling into the ending, I strike a pose at each of four beats, raking a hand along my skirt and over my hair as I arch my back. The place goes nuts.

But then, out comes my competition, and I have every right to be nervous. If you didn't tell me otherwise, I'd say it *is* Britney, this 19-year-old chicklet with legs up to Canada, an utterly fantastic ass, nice rack, big Hollywood lips and a head of hair that rains down in thick ribbons of blondeness. She's a fucking shampoo commercial. The music begins, she vamps to the front of the stage and out comes this voice like an LP played with a concrete needle.

Game over, right? Don't bet on it. Because Britney II has an entourage of fratboys, and it's almost as if she's offered a night of carnal pleasures to whoever yells the loudest. On the first vote, in fact, the ovations are too close to call. But this only serves to piss off my fans even more. A short, bespectacled man jumps in front of his Japanese peers to cheerlead, and when Lani's hand pops open over my head I am blown backward by the loudest, scariest sound I've heard since a Navy air show on Whidbey Island. I am deafened, I am adored, and even a pack of horny fratboys cannot match it. Lani brings the mic to her mouth, declares "I think it's Ruby!" and my fans burst forth in a fugue of coyote yips. My life-long dream of playing Britney Spears has come to pass.

By now you're probably wondering about my talented boyfriend. Unlike me, Harry was no slut for every passing star. He wanted only to be the King. Even though the part of Elvis was the final male audition, making this an all-or-nothing attempt, he would consider no other. As it turned out, his loyalty was richly rewarded – because nobody else tried out. Harry was summarily crowned, and asked to sing "Hound Dog" as proof of his prowess. He was excellent, of course, but I gave him a whack on the butt nonetheless, for the gross inequity of our respective situations.

We spent the next day kayaking – and perhaps that's another reason I got so attached to it. We paddled within the glow of victory, and I could barely hear the sounds of frigate birds, motorboats or waves on rocks with "Hit Me Baby One More Time" playing interminably through my head (without, I might add, the assistance of an IPod). That afternoon, I discovered what a small, magnified community is a cruise ship, and how quickly word of my travails had spread. My biggest fans were the seniors, who relished the fact that someone who sang *their* songs could beat a teenybopper at her own generation's music. Strangers would shout to me in the corridors – "Hey Britney!" "Karaoke girl!" "Go get 'em, Ruby!" – and whenever we came upon my Japanese posse, they weren't happy until I hugged each and every one of them. That night's dinner was a formal-dress affair, and when I entered the hall in my jade-green sequin gown, they *applauded* me. It felt like some wacky Fred Astaire musical, and I ate it up like crème brulee.

You might expect Harry to be taken aback by all of this, perhaps even a little jealous – he was Elvis, after all. But Harry was precisely the opposite, confident enough in his own talent to understand that my four-part battle had become something extraordinary. He had a permanent goofy grin plastered to his mug, and he never tired of telling everybody that he was sleeping with Britney Spears. I think he was also proud that everybody else was finding out about his talented girlfriend, and excited that he would finally get to see me in my element. It didn't hurt when the Japanese contingent would bow down in mock worship and chant "Ellll-vis! Ellll-vis!"

The show was actually pretty easy. They had done it cruise after cruise for God knows how long, and had it carefully programmed for shaky amateurs. After donning our costumes (available in three different sizes), we adjourned to the "green room," which was really just a small landing next to this metallic, Navy-looking stairwell. Harry's Elvis costume – the white Vegas jumpsuit – seemed to turn him into the class cutup, and he went around punching holes in the tension. He turned to Melanie, in her early-Madonna see-through dress, and said, "I hate to mention this, honey, but *we can see your underwear!*" I also remember our lead showgirl, Holly – she of the perfect six-foot body – using the stairway rails to stretch in ways that would probably send the rest of us to the hospital.

Playing the youngest of the icons, I had to wait an interminable amount of time before my escort, a lovely gay dancer named Geoffrey, came to whisk me away. We braced ourselves beside the entrance, elbows coupled, listening for the cue in Britney's intro (I believe it was the word "vixen"), and then he gives me a tug and leads me to a star at center stage. My job is to sing the song without straying from that star, lest I trip up one of the schoolgirls in my "posse," but of course I'm after brownie points. Britney II and her fratboys have every right to be suspicious about the way the same moves I used in my audition are matching up with those of the dancers. The audience just knows, instinctively, that something about my performance is "tighter" than the others. I jolt into that same four-pose ending and freeze with my troupe, taking a loofah shower in the sound of 3,000 hands. It is indescribably sweet.

Geoffrey comes to fetch me back, and we stand in the wings as Harry does his stuff. He definitely has the best production values in the show: the classic *2001: Space Odyssey* intro, followed by a verse of "Hound Dog," followed by "Jailhouse Rock" with a half-dozen twirling babes in Ray-bans and Capri pants. He throws in a couple of leg-waggles and sings his usual excellence, eliding one forgotten phrase with what he calls the Elvis Mumble.

Holly Perfectbody comes to lead him off, and then comes a surprisingly touching elegy: a spotlight on an empty stool as we listen to clips of Sinatra talking about his life. Michael, a journalist from Seattle, comes out in a tux and short-brimmed fedora to sing "My Way" in a voice eerily similar to the original. As the orchestra wells up, the rest of the legends return, and our escorts walk us through a simple choreography. We take our final bows (more loofah, pass the shampoo) and run up the aisle to a nearby lounge for photos. I was tugged away by Harry, who continued talking like Elvis as he kissed away a major portion of my makeup.

"Hey Priscilla, wanna celebrate?"

"And what do you call what you just did?"

"That's just preliminaries, bebe."

"Well first we'd better return these getups."

He ran a hand under the hem of my plaid skirt. "Sure they wouldn't let you keep this just a little longer?"

I had no choice but to squeak like a Mouseketeer. "Mr. Presley! You bad, bad man. I'm gonna tell Colonel Parker on you."

"I'm pretty sure he'd be on my side. Meet me in the Mattress Lounge?"

"That's Matisse, you pedophile."

"Pee-doh… Whassat?"

"Jerry Lee Lewis."

"Oh! Uh-uh-huh."

Harry held my shoulders, keeping me still with those blue eyes, and spoke like Harry again.

"Seriously, Ruby. You were incredible up there. I never dreamed you were that good."

I kissed him thoroughly and sent him off to the men's dressing room with a slap to the hindquarters. He gave me a pistolshot with his fingers, said, "Thankyou. Thankyouvermuch," and joined James Brown in a march backstage.

Between chit-chatting with Aretha and Gloria (silently forgiving them for beating me), receiving my compliments from Geoffrey ("I had you picked out as a pro from square one") and swapping back into my civilian clothes, I was the last one out of the dressing room. When I came back out on stage, the theater was profoundly empty. I have a superstition that goes, Any time you see a mark, hit it, so I ambled up to the star and buried its east and west points under my pumps. A burst of short-term memory washes over me, but it flutters away like a riverbank of butterflies and I arrive at a wall of sadness, as if my veins have all gone indigo. A surge of gravity yanks me seaward, but I fight it, pressing down on that star and turning my legs into treetrunks, letting the tears do what they may.

"Everything OK?"

You could forgive me for thinking it's God – a gruff, booming baritone emanating from stage left. I twist from my star to discover a large man in a double-breasted navy suit. He seems to be in his mid-fifties, balding, with a thick salt-and-pepper beard, but he exudes a virile energy – executive bouncer, high-class Mafioso.

"Stage blues," he says. "You've hit an emotional peak, and now the moment's gone. It's all downhill from here – but at least it's a tall hill."

I perform a few eye rubs to clean the slate.

"No offense, but who the hell are you?"

He lets out a guffaw on a single note, like the ones produced by opera singers during party scenes. "Haw! I'm Albert Camarelli, and I'm quite a fan. You are a marvelous singer."

"Thank you, Mr. Camarelli."

"Please. You can call me Al."

"Al." I take a second to scan the empty seats, trying to put a name to my symptoms. "But you're wrong, Al. I'm familiar with stage blues. I'm a… professional. And I'm wondering why I had to work so *fucking* hard to get this stupid, shitty little part."

"There are no small parts, just…"

"Oh save it, Al!" And here I am, crying again. Al comes over and places a hand on my shoulder.

"I'm sorry. Shouldn't throw cliches at a pro. Would you like to take a walk with me on deck? Just for a few minutes?"

This seems a little forward, but Al's aura emanates benevolence.

"You should know," I say, "I'm already taken."

He smiles. "Everybody knows that. You and Elvis are the golden couple. He's pretty good, too. Nowhere near as good as you."

"I wouldn't say that."

"Honey, there's jazz and then there's the easy stuff. *You're* a jazz singer."

I turn and do a little squeegee job on my face.

"You've heard me sing jazz?"

"All week."

"And I'm a jazz singer?"

"Most definitely."

"Okay, Al. Let's go for a walk."

I take a last, doleful look at my star before following Al up the aisle. The elevator opens on the forward pool area, populated by a few late-night drinkers and a chain-smoking teen in a Ramones T-shirt.

"Britney! You are *hot*, honey."

"Thanks," I say.

We walk a few feet more and Al says, "Feels good, doesn't it?"

I flash him a secret grin. "A teenage boy just called me 'hot,' Al. What do *you* think?"

"Haw! Mind if I puff a stogie? It's a Cuban, so it's now or never."

"Nah. Go ahead."

Al turns away from the breeze, cups his hand and lights up. I wander toward the railing, eyeing the low strip of Baja California, a handful of lights popping from the darkness. Al joins me, proffering his prize.

"Care for a puff?"

"Sure." I twirl the tip in my mouth and take a drag. The smoke carries a rich coffee edge, plus something unexpectedly sweet, like a good port.

"That is lovely," I say.

"You've done this before."

"I've got a friend who smokes Swisher Sweets."

"Egad! On purpose?" He takes it back, tips the ash into a designated container (installed after balcony passengers down below found themselves being attacked by flurries of gray snow), then works the end into an orange glow.

"So! Ruby. Would you play some word association with me?"

"Sure, doc."

"Gershwin."

"But Not For Me."

"Straighten Up and Fly Right."

"Nat King Cole. The trio years."

"Vocalese."

"Take a famous instrumental solo and apply lyrics to it. Created by Lambert, Hendricks and the incomparable Ross."

"Lush Life."

"Ooh! Billy Eckstine. Smokey stuff."

Al stops and turns because he thinks he's got a meaty one.

"Mack the Knife."

"Merry little tune about a serial killer. Kurt Weill, for The Threepenny Opera with Bertolt Brecht. They told him the show needed a prologue to explain the main character; on the way home, he heard a trolley playing that familiar three-note motif: doo doo *doo doo*. Famously recorded by Louis, Ella, Frank and of course Bobby D. Weill also wrote Moon of Alabama, recorded by the Doors, and September Song."

"Um, uh…" Al is running out of steam. "A Small Hotel?"

"Rodgers and Hart. Al? Are we playing Jeopardy?"

He comes to some kind of decision and snaps his fingers. "No. You're *it*, Ruby."

"So we're playing tag? Yaknow, I've really got to meet Elvis in the Matisse…"

"No!" We've arrived at the aft swimming pool. He waves me into a chair. "Just two more minutes, I swear."

I take a seat as Al heads for the bar. He takes out a key and opens a cabinet, then returns with two glasses and a bottle of champagne.

"Al! You're gonna get in trouble."

He gives me a wink. "It's all right. I've got connections." He pops the cork, fills us up and raises a toast. "May you never have to sing Britney Spears ever again."

"You devil! You have come up with something I cannot refuse to drink to."

Al sits down and arranges his legs until he's comfortable, then he leans forward and laces his fingers.

"I've been watching you all week, Ruby. It takes a real connoisseur to know how good you are, and I knew it after three seconds. I spent the rest of the week making sure that I wasn't hallucinating. You have this ability with a song, to mold it, craft it like a fine sculptor – and God forbid, have a little fun with it. What you don't have is this godawful need to flatten out the tone and sap out all the warmth."

"Like Diana Krall?" I ask.

He laughs. "As in, makes my skin Krall. No. You have this marvelous old-fashioned sensibility that never, ever should have gone out of style. Actual vibrato, actual phrasing – call it torch singing, or vocal acting. The seniors appreciate it, because they grew up with it, but only two people on this fucking ship understand precisely what makes it work, and they're both sitting at this table."

I smile and take another sip of Al's very good champagne. "You know, Al? As long as you're not some highly articulate stalker, I could get to like you."

"Haw! That's good, because you might be seeing a lot of me."

"Um… Okay. Why?"

"I'm the vice president of this cruise line, Ruby. I'm also the entertainment director. We get a lot of older passengers on our Alaskan cruises – people who still know and love the great songs. For that and my own purely selfish reasons, I've decided to set up an old-fashioned jazz club, just like the ones you would see in one of those old Astaire movies, and fit it out with a small orchestra and a singer. And I want *you* to be the singer."

Channy

That's about the time I lose it. I slam the table with both hands and yell "No!" spilling half my coffee and alarming the couple at the next table.

"Yes!" says Ruby. "I start next month."

"That is incredible! That is… Oh! Oh Ruby!" I circle the table to give her a hug, and then I grab a handful of napkins to sop up my coffee. It's amazing how quickly my thoughts revert to my own selfish needs.

"But… Does this mean you're leaving?"

"Not at all. The cruises are out of Seattle. A week on/week off kind of thing."

I feel a little dizzy, awash with joy. It's true – empathy is a workable drug. But I've got one more doubt.

"Is this… Is this enough for you?"

Ruby tents her fingers. "I believe the quote was, I will no longer chase a dream that doesn't chase me. Well honey, this particular dream stalked me for a week and then toasted me with champagne and Cuban cigars! And I think by now I've got a handle on my basic needs. I need to stand in front of people and sing to them. If it's on a cruise ship, an entire country away from Times Square, then so be it!"

We both relax into our chairs, chewing our perfect bread. Ruby lets out little aspirations of wonder left over from the Mexican Pacific. Then she snaps to and raps her knuckles on the table.

"Oh, Channy. Me me me! I completely forgot – did you hear anything about Kai?"

Don't think I'm not tempted. I have huge, carnivorous creatures crawling inside of me, and if I don't expose them to the light of day they will eat me alive. But I am not about to rain on such a spectacular parade.

"Nope," I say. "Haven't heard a thing."

The Shape Poem

In a shape poem, a poet uses the lines of his text to form the silhouette of an identifiable visual image – generally, an image that represents or comments upon the subject of the poem.

The shape poem goes back to Greek Alexandria of the third century B.C., when poems were written to be presented on objects such as an ax handle, a statue's wings, an altar – even an egg. English poet George Herbert (1593-1633) led an Elizabethan movement using shape poems strictly for the page: two examples are "Easter Wings" and "The Altar," written in the shape of, yes, wings and an altar. Lewis Carroll toyed with the notion in *Alice's Adventures in Wonderland*, presenting "The Mouse's Tale" in the shape of a mouse's tail. The form continued into the 20th century through the typographical experiments of F.T. Marinetti and his anarchistic Futurism movement, Guillaume Apollinaire's 1918 *Calligrammes* collection, the playful tinkering of e.e. cummings, the Chinese ideograms used by Ezra Pound, and various works by members of the Dadaist movement.

In the 1950s, a group of Brazilian poets led by Carlos Drummond de Andrade and Augusto de Campos sought to fully integrate the dual role of words as carriers of language and visual art. Using a phrase coined by European artists Max Bill and Öyvind Fahlström, the Brazilian group declared themselves the "concrete poetry" movement. In 1958, they issued a fiery manifesto lamenting the use of "words as mere indifferent vehicles, without life, without personality, without history, taboo-tombs in which convention insists on burying the idea."

Concrete poetry was originally aimed at using words in an abstract manner, without an allusion to identifiable shapes. But as the movement reached the height of its popularity in the 1960s, it became less abstract and was adopted by conventional poets as a specific poetic form rather than a full visual/literary fusion. Many of them returned to the shape-based forms popular in the third century B.C.

Among the best of the '60s shape poets was John Hollander, who created his works with a typewriter. As a scholar, editor and accomplished poet – working in many different forms – Hollander also provided a thorough explication of the process in his 1969 collection *Types of Shape*. Hollander described his process in a 2003 interview with the *St. John's University Humanities Review:*

"I would think of the representation of some object in silhouette – a silhouette which wouldn't have any holes in it – and then draw the outlines, fill in the outlines with typewriter type … and then contemplate the resulting image for anywhere from an hour to several months. The number of characters per line of typing would then give me a metrical form for the lines of verse, not syllabic but graphematic (as a linguist might put it). These numbers, plus the number of incidents from flush left, determined the form of each line of the poem."

In Hollander's 1969 "Swan and Shadow," he uses the text to create the silhouette of a swan, the surface of a lake and the swan's upside-down shadow. Hollander relates the words of the poem to their physical location within the image. (The swan's head, for example, describes "Dusk / Above the / water…").

"One certainly needs no artistic talent in order to draw a good bit, and certainly not to rough out a silhouette," Hollander says. "It's not a lack of talent, but an absolutely dreadful educational system that prevents everyone from being able to draw a little."

Making the Poem

Through laborious trial-and-error experiments, I've devised a process for creating a shape poem, with two inherent biases. First, my process gives precedence to preserving the integrity of the original poem, applying the visual image afterward. Second, my process takes advantage of two modern advances: the image reduction/enlargement capabilities of today's copiers, and the convenience offered by computer word-processing programs.

Write a Poem. Try free verse or prose forms.

Imagine a Shape. It doesn't have to reflect the primary subject of the poem. Sometimes it's more effective to choose a shape that reflects a small detail or provides a subtle comment on the discourse.

Find an Image. In addition to the Internet, you might try magazines, photo books, children's coloring books or craft stores.

Get the Right Size. Run the lines of your poem together, inserting punctuation as needed, and print it out as a single prose paragraph. Compare the area taken up by your poem and that provided by your image. Use a copy machine to reduce or enlarge the image accordingly.

Cut and Paste. Cut your poem into one-line strips and paste them over your image with a glue stick, beginning each line at the left margin of the image, and ending it at or slightly past the right margin. If you run out of words before you run out of image – or vice versa – return to the copier, adjust your image size and cut and paste again. This is the most arduous step, but it'll make the final two steps much easier.

Head to Your Computer. Identify your most leftward line. Beginning at flush left, type the entire line; then work your way upward and downward, using your space bar to position each line's first letter according to its relationship to adjoining letters.

Edit. Once you've typed out the poem, you may want to adjust or change the words to polish the silhouette.

Waltz in Red

In the novel *Outro*, Ruby Cohen tells karaoke hostess Channy about her life as an Off-Broadway actress in New York – and some of the characters she met along the way.

Three years later, I was still with Joe's troupe, Greenstreet Productions, alternating between big roles and small, fending off anything that smacked of administrative duties. I displayed my kryptonite competence only when it came to knowing my lines, arriving punctually and performing with every cell in my body. I did, however, have an intriguing proposition in my pocket: Joe had invited me to direct one of the shows for the upcoming season. It was tempting but scary, because I knew I'd be good at it and I didn't want anything to come between me and the audience.

It was late summer, down-time before the fall opening. I found a flyer for an artists' collective at a bar around the corner – a place called Savvy's. When I walked in, the mood was positively Beatnik. The garret from Puccini's *Boheme*. Andy Hardy putting on a show in the barn.

I swam through the bar crowd until I reached a wide pit where a funk band was wrapping up "Sex Machine," a skinny black guy in a British cap spazzing a James Brown shuffle across the floor. Then the DJ called up a slam poet, a short, squat guy with a Fiddler-on-the-Roof beard. He jumped into a piece about trying to eliminate the excess food from his pantry, and instead winding up in an eating competition with Death. The rhythm of his words accelerated with a Bolero graduality until they caught fire and burst into a Ginsbergian inventory of comestibles. People were falling out of their chairs, probably on purpose.

By the time he was done, a reggae band had finished setting up, and rolled into a Jimmy Cliff tune. I took the opportunity to saunter up to the balcony, where a trio of painters were doing "live works." A large black woman was pressing broad swipes of acrylic across a canvas, setting up the strata for a seascape. A baby-faced Puerto

Rican kid scratched at a charcoal portrait: an old drunk leaning against a bar, wearing a look of utter dejection.

The third guy was older, mid-thirties, tall, a head of thick black hair with apostrophes of gray. He looked like he had never made an awkward movement in his life. He was working on a cartoonish, beatific creature with fan-shaped wings – or petals, I couldn't tell. It stood upon a pedestal-like body, wide as a tree trunk. The background was an intricate network of lines, but looking closely I could see that it was actually composed of faces, their features melting into the mass: an Aztec warrior in profile, an amoeba with misplaced Picasso eyes, a robot alien with a saucer-shaped head.

The man was dipping a terry-cloth rag into a bowl of raw sienna paint, then scrubbing it into one of the petals – or wings. He gave me a quick glance, but kept steadily at his work. For a moment, I felt guilty for distracting him, but of course that's what he was there for. And, to answer stupid questions.

"Whatcha doin'?"

He looked up with eyes so black you could fall right in. "You want the short version or the Encyclopedia Britannica?"

"Um… I'm gonna go for the short."

"We begin with a central figure: the ruby-throated angelflower. A profoundly positive presence. I filled in the background with a coterie of beer-coaster creatures, then sort of macramed them together in order to, in order to… Actually, I have no idea."

"To make them look like a crowd?"

He snapped his fingers very loudly, then stared at them in surprise. "Wow – what's *that* about? But yes! A crowd. Out of which rises the angelflower, like the rare and sudden blossoming of the century plant, erupting from the desert of the hoi polloi.

"I have this thing about complicated backgrounds. I get so attached to a project that I hate to see it end – so all this meticulous stuff helps to extend the work. Right now you've caught me at the final step, which is frankly like a three-year-old with a coloring book. I like to water down my acrylics, then scrub them in. Gives a nice solid block of color – but transparent, so it reveals the flaws in the canvas."

"Why do you want to reveal flaws?"

"I like a surface that's seen some livin'. This one was a dropcloth. Note the little splatters of black at the top of the stem. That was an oil change."

He took another swab at his bowl and worked a corner of the petal, drawing the paint right up to the thick black line at its periphery.

"I can't stand art that's too smooth. If you're not going to reveal the process at all, then why bother? This notion of creating perfect, untouched forms is riven with hubris. What are you doing after the show?"

He said all of this at a shot, and I wasn't entirely certain that I'd been asked a question.

"Um, I don't really know."

"I have to show you something."

I laughed. "Don't think I've never heard *that* one before."

He took my hand and held on tight, as if we were about to shake on a deal.

"What's your name?"

"Ruby."

He smiled. Large, dazzling teeth. "You see?"

"Ruby-throated," I said. "As in fate?"

"As in coincidence – which is better, and tastier. *You* are one of the special ones. You do something creative?"

"So now you're a psychic?"

He laughed. "Ask the right question in the right milieu, and your odds are pretty good."

"Yes," I said. "Actress."

"Ah – of course. Lots of personalities swimming around in there. When you first came up, I thought there was a whole mob watching me. I'll be done at midnight. Can I meet you at the bar?"

"What? I can't watch you?"

"Actually, no. I'd be too distracted. Along with being one of the special ones, you're enormously attractive."

Picture me as an LP on a turntable; my needle has just been yanked away. I tried and failed to fight down a goofy smile.

"Wait a minute," I said. "What's *your* name?"

"Scootie." He shook the hand I'd forgotten he was holding. "And yes, there's a story behind that, too. But I need to get back to my painting."

He let go, and I drifted downstairs. I gave some serious thought to leaving – he was entirely too smooth. But this cool punk band was playing, dressed in big chunks of black and white fabric, and a beer sounded really good.

Two bands and a standup comic later, Scootie appeared over my left shoulder, continuing our previous conversation as if we'd never stopped.

"When I was a baby, I had a middle ear infection. It messed up my sense of balance, and I took to crawling sideways, like a crab. So I got my nickname: 'Scootie'. Have you done any Beckett?"

I fixed him with a look, and attempted to restart the conversation in a more normal fashion. "Hi, Scootie. How ya doin'?"

He blinked. "I'm fine. How are you?"

"Good! *Waiting for Godot*."

You could see that little tidbit striking a speed-bump in his head – which was exactly my intention.

"Isn't that…?"

"All-female cast," I said. "We thought of calling it *Waiting for Goddess*, but we figured we were pushing our luck as it was."

The bartender raced by, planted a Heinekin in front of Scootie, spoke the words "Jacks and Queens" and kept going.

Scootie eyed the label, said "Ah, Jacks and Queens," and took a drink. "What did you think of it?" he asked.

"Jacks and Queens?"

"Beckett."

I did my best to look thoughtful (I'm sure I did – I had practiced my "thoughtful" look in a mirror many times). "Irrational. Maddening. Plotless. Ridiculous. I *loved* it."

"You ought to love me then."

"Umm… maybe?" Keep it moving, keep it moving. "So where do your figures come from?"

"John Cage."

"Oh. I thought Cage was a musician."

"You thought Da Vinci was a painter. Music was Cage's day job. When the moon came out, he was a philosopher. And the master cartographer of chance operations."

Scootie took a pen from behind his ear and flipped over a beer coaster. Then he drew a long line, vaguely ess-shaped.

"I can't illustrate worth shit. Any time I attempt to pull in something from the real world, it goes through some kind of crippling filter and ends up looking like the work of an unimaginative toddler. So I go backwards."

He drew a straight line through the ess at a slant.

"I keep drawing lines until something makes itself known."

A question mark with no period. Three sides of a square, facing down.

"When I arrive at the point of identity, I finish the job with universal signifiers: eyes, nose, mouth – sometimes ears, or hair."

He gave the question-mark head a pair of almond-shaped eyes, then angled a mouth-line with a small notch for a smirk. The nose was already there, a product of the first two lines. The upside-down square offered a torso; he added long, thin rectangles to imply arms.

"Sometimes they turn out, sometimes not. Sometimes they become ruby-throated angelflowers."

"This one looks French," I said. "That smirk might actually be a cigarette."

Scootie smiled, initialed the coaster *SJ* and handed it to me.

"Here. Might be worth a dollar someday."

He had a loft (of *course* he had a loft). It was pretty bare of furniture, and instead of a rug he had a canvas dropcloth, ten foot square, nailed to the floor. Affixed to the far wall was a canvas, five feet tall, three wide. It appeared to contain a swarm of mosquitoes, but closer inspection revealed words, hundreds of them, written with a black marker. I saw *libretto, 1967,* and *Sutherland.*

"What the hell is going on here?"

"Chance operations," he said. "The human mind craves organization – and that's the problem. I was in a choir once, singing a piece that called for white noise, within a certain range of pitches. Inevitably, we would gravitate toward consonance – toward chords. So we had to spend a half-hour assigning individual pitches to individual singers. There were some who hated that piece, but I thought it was the most beautifully constructed chaos I'd ever heard.

"The thing is, in order to achieve true randomness, you have to set up some ground rules beforehand. In this case, I determined to take the *New Grove Book of Opera* – all 687 pages – and extract the first word from each page. On the canvas, I depended on my natural ability to shuffle, beginning with any available white space and not caring if it ran roughshod over other words. I wanted a virtual windstorm of verbiage. Unbeknownst to you, I have already pencilled in the central figure, and will now bring him into being. Please – sit."

He handed me a cushion, and I sat on the floor, cross-legged. He produced a small housepainting brush, dipped it into a jar of black paint and drew a rough line over the canvas. He began with two lines that started at the top center and extended outward. He drew a vee from one shoulder to another, trailing into a shape that resembled a tie. At either side of the X, he affixed the same almond eyes as his coaster creature, then a wide, flat oval for a mouth, vaguely merry. He stood back for a moment, then dipped the brush, took the tips of the X and extended them to the upper corners. He took a last look, notched a pocket on either side of the tie, then tossed the brush over his shoulder. It landed on the dropcloth with a splat. Then he knelt behind me, gripped my shoulders and said, "So. What is he?"

I took a few moments to study.

"The Creature from the Black Lagoon in a business suit."

"Or a suit for the opera," said Scootie.

"But those antennae…?"

"Yes! That popped in just now."

"Like a cockroach. A giant impresario cockroach, off to the opera."

"Luciano Cucaracchi," he said.

I let out a burst of laughter, like a sneeze. "Okay."

"Hey, I don't make up the names. They just come in on the satellite dish. Now, take off your shoes."

There was my decision point. A girl doesn't take off her shoes just for anyone.

So I did. Scootie disappeared and came back with a pair of square plastic tubs. In one he poured red paint, in the other black.

"It's just like roullette. Pick a color."

I stood up and gave them a study. "Dare I ask why?"

"Ask yourself this question: what color do I want my feet to be for the next week?"

"You're nuts."

"We've established that. Now pick."

"Red. Of course."

"Communist!"

"Vampire!"

"Go ahead. Do the Hokey-Pokey."

I knew if I thought about it, I wouldn't, so I didn't think about it. I don't need to tell you how it felt, because you know how it felt. Scootie pushed a button on his stereo and conjured a waltz – that soprano from *Boheme*, in the café. He rolled his trousers to his knees, planted himself in the black, then left a trail of dance-instruction footprints on his way to the center of the dropcloth. He raised his hands; I stepped forward and took them.

And he could waltz (of course he could waltz). And of course *I* could waltz – I was a performer. We stopped at regular intervals to reload our feet. After that came Sinatra, "Saturday Night is the Loneliest Night of the Week," and we switched to swing. Scootie's lead was perfect, all the signals there in his big hands, twirling me one way, wrapping me the other. At the ending, he dipped me so deeply that, the next morning, I found streaks of red and black in my hair.

Scootie pulled me to my feet, kissed my hands and said, "We're done."

I stood on red tip-toes, kissed him on the neck and said, "Not hardly."

"All drama is about dissonance. All comedy is about dissonance. Where would we be without the sword and the banana peel?"

--Bruce Adolphe, composer

What's My Line?

The right profession for your characters will open up a wealth of possibilities in your story. Do your research and create an authentic feel for a protagonist's vocation.

First published in Writer's Digest

Here's the situation: You're at a party. You've just met someone. Names are exchanged – and then you face the daunting task of beginning a conversation. What are the next words out of your mouth?

"So – what do you do?"

Why is this? Simple – because a person's job provides a readily accessible, non-invasive point of inquiry that is rife with conversational possibilities. That one tidbit can inspire common ground, follow-up questions, insights on character, avenues to humor – possibly even free advice.

"Action *is* character," wrote Fitzgerald – and few actions speak louder than what we choose to do for a living.

Employ your characters! Even when career factors are far from the main thrust of your narrative, carefully choosing and researching occupations for your fictional heroes opens up a wealth of possibilities for enriching your story. Let's look at how some of today's best authors have done just that:

Framing the Point-of-View

In David Guterson's 1999 novel, *East of the Mountains*, elderly widower Ben Givens discovers that he's dying of colon cancer. His reaction to this news is largely determined by one important fact: Givens is a retired heart surgeon.

Like all physicians, he knew the truth of such a verdict; he knew full well the force of cancer and how inexorably it operated. He grasped that nothing could stop his death, no matter how hopeful he allowed himself to feel, no matter how deluded... Better to end his life swiftly, cleanly, and to accept that there would be no thwarting the onslaught of the disease.

By making his protagonist a doctor, Guterson sets up the philosophical framework for his hero's quest: finding the best way to die. He also provides the opportunity for Givens to keep the disease a secret, and, thereby, to make his suicide look like an accident.

Making Work the Story (Making the Story Work)

In his 1993 collection, *Working Men*, Michael Dorris uses work not just as a point of reference, but often as the central conflict. In the story "Jeopardy," drug salesman Don Banta's main task – obtaining physician signatures acknowledging their conversations – means that he spends most of his waking hours chit-chatting medical receptionists. His first target is Dee Dee, whose son suffers from allergies.

"Lots of pollen around, huh? Hey, maybe your little boy... That's not him in the frame on your desk? I can't believe how he's grown. No... Maybe he could try this new inhaler. It's a miracle worker. Just remember, you don't know where you got it, right, because I could get in major trouble and it's just because we're friends, you know, and I had allergies myself as a kid."

All in all, a pathetic existence, brought to a devastating nadir when Banta learns that his father has died. Stuck in a motel room with no one to talk to, he calls Dee Dee – and learns that the inhaler he used to bribe his way into her office has saved her son from a near-fatal allergy attack.

Establishing Character

In Anne Tyler's 1985 novel, *Accidental Tourist*, Macon Leary is suffering from his son's murder, his subsequent divorce, and his dog Edward's growing inclination for biting people. Although dog trainer Muriel Pritchett appears in the story-space usually reserved for a love interest, her loony verbal flights hardly seem a match for a fragile, phobic intellectual. But Muriel trains Edward with a fierce competence, and tells some amazing stories – like the day she was knocked down by a Doberman Pinscher:

"Come to find him standing over me, showing all his teeth. Well, I thought of what they said at Doggie, Do: Only one of you can be boss. So I tell him, 'Absolutely not.' ...and my right arm is broken so I hold out my left, hold out my palm and stare into his eyes – they can't stand for you to meet their eyes – and get to my feet real slow. And durned if that dog doesn't settle right back on his haunches."

"Good Lord," Macon said.

Painting a Canvas

In Annie Proulx's 1993 novel, *The Shipping News*, Quoyle returns to his ancestral home in Newfoundland, and gets a job at the local paper, covering the boats coming in to harbor. Giving Quoyle this particular assignment allows Proulx to tap into the town's *raison d'etre*, as well as the delicious patois of the seagoing trade, like this passage from a local boatbuilder:

"There's the backbone of your boat, She's scarfed now. You glance at that, somebody who knows boats, you can see the whole thing right there. But there's nobody can tell 'ow she'll fit the water, handle in the swells and lops until you try 'er out. Except poor old Uncle Les, Les Budgel. Dead now... Built beautiful skiffs and dories, butter on a 'ot stove."

Proulx adds to this canvas by heading her chapters with diagrams and descriptions of sailor's knots.

The secret to all of these is that they feel *authentic* – as if the author himself has performed this line of work. It's possible to capture some of this by reading – but reading is only a start. What you really need is first-hand experience, and real-life sources. Following are some strategies that have worked for me:

Use Ur Own

Sad to say, if you're writing fiction, you've probably got a day job. Why not use it? And don't discount the non-glamorous. A lot of your readers will have much more in common with a shipping clerk than a shipping magnate.

Squeezed into a grimy crawl space, soldering copper pipes for my contractor brother-in-law, I began to notice the small, poetic details: the horizontal ballet of positioning the torch, the way the lead solder flashed around the joint as it melted, the pleasing hiss when I ran a damp rag over the hot pipe. I decided to give this same assignment to the poet-protagonist of my novel, *Rhyming Pittsburgh*, hoping to complicate the effete-intellectual stereotype with a healthy dose of blue-collar grit.

Upgrade a Hobby

Lots of hobbies are simply professions performed on an amateur level. Easy enough, then, to take the knowledge attained as a hobbyist and "crank it up" to the level of a fictional pro.

In the nineties, I played drums for several rock and blues bands. Although I never got to the pro level, I *met* a lot of pros, played a few clubs, and got a good, all-around feel for the musician's life. I've since had two drummer-protagonists (one in a play, one in a novel), made plentiful use of backstage stories, and even filled out the details with specific musical passages from my playing days.

Be a Journalist

Ask questions. Be a buttinsky. People love to talk about their jobs – especially if you tell them you're working on a novel.

But hey – why not get *paid* to be a buttinsky? Local papers are always on the lookout for stories on interesting residents and their vocations. And being "on assignment" gives you that much more license to snoop.

For my opera novel, *Gabriella's Voice*, I set up an extensive research program. I got an assignment reviewing the San Francisco Opera. I took a soprano friend out to dinner, parked a tape recorder next to her silverware and asked her three hours' worth of questions. Then I spent a full season with her company, hanging out at auditions, rehearsals and cast parties, picking up backstage stories.

The reviews I most enjoy from *Gabriella* come from singers, who spend half the book laughing at all the inside jokes, and inevitably come back to me with that priceless question, "How did you *know* all that?"

The "Life-Line" Strategy

Another thing I learned from *Gabriella* – this from the editing process – is that it's easy to carry your research too far, and bury your story in technical details (as if to say, Hey! Look at all the research I did!"). An effective way to fight this off is to establish a correspondence with a real-life expert, and get your information on an "as-needed" basis (similar to the "Life Line" option on the game show "Who Wants to Be a Millionaire?").

For my novel, *Double Blind*, I wanted the particular world-view of a scientist – and just happened to have a friend, Rob, who works as a geneticist.

One typical transaction went like this: I wrote, "My character is doing one last thing before leaving work at the end of the day. What is it?" Rob wrote back, "Running his gels," and described a process for preserving tumor samples. In this case, however, the details were unnecessary. I was simply moving my character from one setting to the next, and needed only that simple three-word phrase, "running his gels," to add a note of authenticity.

You can also use your Life Line later, to proofread your manuscript for technical errors.

The Prescient Literary/Vocational Advantages of Anticipatory Experiential Ventures

I once had a playwright friend – inveterate spewer of writerly slogans – who used to say, "You gotta *live* before you can *write*." This is the final thought I'd like to leave you with. Though it's great to use your character's occupation as an excuse to dig up first-hand experiences, the reverse is also true: You ought to pursue these kinds of adventures at all times, with the idea that, someday later, you'll use them in your writing.

It's not just a good way to approach fiction. It's a good way to approach *life*.

Mustang Sally

Call her a red-haired Jewish soul eyed brick wall Los Angeles blues belter wide stance evil eye coffee espresso stare melt you into the sidewalk. You needn't say more unless you feel like it.

Big Irish lug nut sits on the ride cymbal, too lost in his two four fills to hear
the singer, nothing more than a shoulder blade on his middle tom.

Still, two days later he draws the picture in full fashion: shafts of sun piping the next door brickpile; longneck Buds, a shower of smoke, guitar case coffins; stage stack of Clapton drivers, one China rip and roll sax.

Mustang Sally holds up a strong pale hand, cantering the tempo. The band stays rutstuck lagging, but not me, me and my high hat frills. I follow her fingers all the way down with the cue of my sticks: twelve bars, twelve bars and home.

The Beast Has Eight Beats

In the novel *The Monkey Tribe*, life coach Benjamin Haas decides that the main thing plaguing his client, unemployed accountant Jack Teagarden, is an inability to see the full range of the possible lives he might pursue. In order to open up his mind, Ben takes Jack to a drum-circle party, where he orders him to smoke his first-ever dose of marijuana.

It seems to take forever for the pot to take hold, but just about the time that Jack is having this thought he realizes that he actually *is* stoned. It feels like he's walking around underwater, without the need for oxygen – or maybe he has gills, how cool would *that* be? Every few minutes, he seems to punch back through to his normal consciousness, and each time he finds himself in a new physical location, as if he's undergoing some kind of teletransportation. During one of these, he finds himself having an animated conversation with Constance over the idea of voluntary evolution, and he finds that his brain has separated into two discrete camps. One camp takes what Constance has said and spits back new ideas in complex, cogent combinations ("It could be that computerized intelligence is the ultimate tool that we have developed for intentionally advancing the mass intelligence"). The other camp appears in the form of a coffeehouse slacker, coolly smoking a clove cigarette and saying, "Dude! How are you even *doing* this? You are *so stoned*!"

"And then there's this constant, individual search for identity. Are we really defined by our jobs, or the ways in which each of us cultivates our intelligence and, thereby, our spiritual selves?"

This is Constance. The tone of her voice is simultaneously soft and firm, a dichotomy that Jack finds intriguing. Did he just think the word *dichotomy*?

"I mean, look at your case. That is *so* fucked up that you have to go through all that stuff just because some cold-blooded corporation has to send another thousand jobs overseas."

"Oh God! And the really screwed-up part is…" (This seems to be Jack's own voice, which sounds oddly loose and vibrant, like a morning-radio DJ.) "…the fucking bastard who cost me my job got off scot-free. And now he's letting me stay at his beach house while he's off on vacation. But *that's* only because I caught him cheating on his wife in Oregon. You ever hear of the Devil's Horns? Or Multnomah Falls? In fact, this *house* has its own waterfall. Crazy, high-tech haunted mansion. Scares the hell out of me."

"Dude!" says the slacker. He picks at the fresh rattlesnake tattoo on his arm. "Why the *hell* are you telling her all this? Was that a drum?"

Jack teletransports again, surfacing on an easy chair as a black cat purrs at his shoulder. The stereo is playing an African tribe before the big hunt, thin, coal-black men jumping around a fire in Picasso masks. To his left he finds the moon goddess Terra, one ear cocked to a round frame drum painted with an Irish knot. She holds a stick with bulbous tips on either end, shaking it back and forth across the skin to produce a rolling thunder. Above and behind her is Constance, wearing a focused expression as she works her hands over two standing drums – he believes these are congas.

Across the room, Ivan stands with a cylindrical drum tied around his waist, rolling his hands across the top. The rolls are incredibly rapid, creating high bursts of sound that ride the top of the rumble like a surfer at the peak of a wave. Sitting just behind Ivan is Ben, sipping calmly from a pint of Guinness. He sets it down, then picks up a dark, lacquered frog and runs a stick along its ridged back, producing a sound very much like a frog. ("Genius!" says the slacker.) Ben scans the room, one player at a time, mapping the sonic layout.

The front door opens, admitting a red flame with green cat's-eyes. Willie jumps from behind his bongos to perform a greeting dance, gray goat's hooves tied around his ankles. The red flame gives birth to a smile, and scarlet lips that kiss Willie on his plump cheek.

Jack looks down and realizes that he is holding a drum between his knees, a smaller version of Ivan's. The drum carries a circle of dark fur around its rim, held tight by a fishnet of knots and strings. Jack follows the grain of the skin, swirls of butterscotch and chocolate against a field of sepia. The swirls are like words in a sentence; when he reaches the period, he thumps it with a finger. The drum gives out a hollow sound like black Peruvian coffee. The sound shakes all the way to his legbones, exiting out his toes, which are tapping to the beat of the tribe. He strikes the period with his palm and the sound nearly spills him from his chair. Jack smiles.

An hour later, they're still at it. Jack's hands begin to ache from the unaccustomed abuse. He scans the room to find his comrades intent on their work, their eyes settled on a middle space over their drumheads, driving the great rumbling beast forward. And yet, it's the beast that's truly in charge, like an enormous dog dragging its owner by a leash. Despite the physical distances between the drummers, they are closer in this conversation, this negotiation of rhythm, than if they were speaking face-to-face.

Jack's hands are doing things that he really doesn't understand; he has no idea where this ability might have come from. But on he goes, playing along the drumhead even as he finds the red flame directly across from him, seated on a low stool with a drum just like his. She flashes her green cat's eyes, and appears to be sending him a message. It arrives in a single thump, and although Jack doesn't get it, his hands do. He waits for the beast to circle back to that same place in time and sends the single thump right back. Flame girl grins, revealing a leftward quirk in her thick, pliable lips. She waits again on the beast and sends out two beats. ("It's a djembe," says the slacker. "You're both playing djembes.") Jack's hands follow the circle and strike the same two. The two of them keep adding beats until they reach eight, and the beast can hold no more. *The beast has eight beats!* If you play two beats, you have to wait six more till the circle returns. If you play three, you wait five, four/four, one/seven. Numbers! No one told him there would be numbers. He sends the red flame a loopy grin, excuses himself from their tennis match and sets off into a roll, fractions too small to count, stirring up the blurred light with his fingers.

Jack hears an off-beat beneath the rumble and tracks the sound to the far side of the room, where Ivan sits behind a pair of white drums carved with Chinese calligraphy. He drives them forward with two padded mallets, stepping out of his pattern to hammer the two big beats. Jack's hands are talking to him; they say, 'It's another message.' The two beats begin to spread around the circle, making new converts, growing in volume, gathering silent space around themselves until they are sonic booms, shaking the walls. Ivan flairs the mallets over his head, a gesture that says, *Get ready.* The beast circles once more and down they come, followed by a hacked-off silence that sucks the air out of the room. The tribe answers with a thrilled chorus of laughter, shouting, Mexican gritos, a few stomps on the floor. Jack makes a sound like an overstimulated crow. The ruckus smooths out into a river of chatter: "That ending! What a I *love* that part where you Did you see Ivan *dude!* You were going *off* little clicking thing God! I'm so I mean awesome! I don't believe we've met."

A small white hand, palms red with use. He follows it up the arm to a porcelain face, cat's eyes, red flame of hair.

"Hi," says Jack.

"Yes you are. What's your name, sailor?"

"Jack."

"No. That's the dog."

"No, no," says Jack, then loses himself in a fit of giggling.

Ben's face appears between them. "No, it really is Jack. Jack, this is Audrey, the bird lady of Monterey."

"She's fucking gorgeous," says Jack, who is completely unaware that he has just spoken these words out loud.

"Ha!" Audrey laughs. "Smooth talker."

"No, believe me, really," says Jack. "Not talking smooth ever."

"Okayee." Audrey looks to Ben. "First-timer?"

Ben laughs huskily. "For everything: drumming, pot, hookah pipe…"

"Hookah pipe!" says Audrey. "Where?"

"Follow me," says Ben. "You too, Jack."

"Right," says Jack – but Jack's intentions are immediately derailed by the smell of egg rolls. He discovers an entire tray of them on the table, steaming with heat, and attacks them like a bear waking from hibernation. This causes a white flame of laughter from his left. It's Terra, her face glistening with sweat from the drumming.

"I don't know why the munchies are so funny," she says. "They just *are*. After you're done gorging yourself, young man, Ben says you should go back toward the car and you'll spot him. And if you need some extra incentive, Audrey'll be there, too."

"Are those deviled eggs?" says Jack. "And sushi! Oh my God."

After consuming an enormous quantity of food, Jack grabs a chocolate brownie and makes for the front door. The lawn is dark again, and two tall, gangly men are slashing at each other with light sabers, each of them holding a can of beer in his free hand. Jack spots the dull white ghost of Ben's Miata and heads down the walk. Hearing hoarse laughter from the carport, he rounds the corner to find Willie and Constance roasting marshmallows over a trio of logs in a tiny barbecue grill. Beyond them is a shimmering blue light that smells like strawberries. It's a hot tub, with three occupants: Ivan, Ben and Audrey. Ben calls out.

"Jack! Over here, lad. Have a dip and a smoke. Or a smoke and a dip."

"Or a doke," says Ivan.

"Or a smip," says Audrey.

Ben inserts the tip of a long, thin hose into his mouth and releases a cloud of smoke. The hose trails back to a tall object on a nearby picnic table, looking like the kind of lamp that sometimes contains genies. The lamp wears a cap of aluminum foil, bearing two ash-gray bars with glowing orange hearts.

"Jack," says Ben. "Is that chocolate on your teeth?"

"Yes!" says Jack.

"The brownies next to the deviled eggs?"

"I think so. Why?"

Ben taps a thoughtful finger against his cheek, then smiles. "I'll... tell you later. So, are you coming in?"

"But...I don't have a bathing suit."

"Well that certainly didn't stop *us*."

It's about this time that Jack notices Audrey's breasts, small milk-white mounds with strawberry-colored nipples. He feels his face growing hot.

Ben takes another puff and hands the pipe to Audrey. He gives Jack a serious study. "I'm sorry, Jack. It could be I'm pushing you too hard. Lord knows, you have so far been a tremendously pleasant surprise. You were *terrific* on the drums."

"Numbers," says Jack. "It's all numbers."

"So it is! That's marvelous, Jack. You are a certified public accountant of rhythm. However, I fear that you will miss out on this delicious feeling, of sitting naked in a hot tub with nothing but your friends and the stars! Let's see, where *is* that switch." He finds a dial on the side of the tub and turns off the underwater lamps. All that remains is a flickering light from the barbecue.

"Now's your chance, Jack!" says Audrey. "Take it off, baby!"

Something about a gorgeous female commanding him to strip makes Jack laugh out loud; he decides to further the gag by pretending he's actually going to do it.

"Okay. But only if everyone closes their eyes."

"Fine," says Ben. "But you only get ten seconds. Ten… nine…"

It's a part of Jack's corporate nature that he simply cannot resist a deadline. He tears off his jeans, shirt and underwear, then vaults over the side of the tub with such haste that he almost slips and falls. He settles into a space between Ivan and Audrey, submerging his private parts just before Ben calls out zero and switches on the lights. His tubmates open their eyes, snickering.

Audrey smiles in a most adorable fashion. "Where do you find these babes in the wood, Ben?"

"Coffeehouses. This one was eavesdropping on one of my sessions and found me simply irresistible. Now, my student prince. You've come this far, you may as well try the hookah. Are you sure it was the brownies next to the deviled eggs?"

"I think so."

"Okay, now this smokes just like a cigarette, and it won't make you cough like the pot."

Jack accepts the pipe-end from Audrey, trying hard to keep his eyes on her face. He holds the end in his teeth and breathes in. It's a sweet smoke, vapor chewing gum, and he realizes it tastes like strawberries.

"It's a flavored tobacco," says Ben. "Very smooth."

"Dude! Check *that* out." Ivan gestures over the back fence. A sliver of moon is creeping past the ridgeline, a silver cap on the dark east hills. Audrey leans toward Jack to say something, which makes him that much more conscious of his nakedness. But he has to admit, the nakedness feels good. It's not so much a sexual thing as a sense that he has crossed a line and now is dangling off the edge of the world, utterly unfettered, in a terrified sort of way. He also can't believe he's just had all of these thoughts in the time that it takes Audrey to lean his way.

"I hate to admit that I peeked," she says. "But I couldn't help noticing that you forgot to take off your socks."

In such close quarters, her whisper may as well be an aria. Ivan and Ben burst into laughter. Jack practices a rough yoga attempting to remove said socks without revealing his privates. He lifts them like a pair of used condoms and tosses them to the cement with a dull splop.

The laughter dies down; Ivan manages to ignite a joint and send it around the tub. Jack smokes it without coughing, and feels sophisticated. The talking dies down in the dance of fireflame, stars sprinkled like grains of sugar on a pitch-black table. Jack feels that his synapses have been lain open to the night, and a thought enters the stream like the taste of a strawberry: *This must be something like what they mean when they say "happiness."* He feels Audrey's fingers folding around his.

"What's interesting about acting is playing characters you're *not* like."

    --Molly Ringwald, actor

Pedro and Angelina

From the novel *Frosted Glass* (Dead End Street, LLC)

In the lovely orchard lands of Oregon's Hood River Valley, in the shadow of the diamond white volcano, there lived a proud and prosperous grower of pear trees named Esteban Ochoas. Esteban possessed a generous, joyous spirit, but one forever marked by the loss of his wife, Lucia, ten years before. Lucia had perished in a car accident, forced off a snowy mountain road by an out-of-control big rig. Ever since that morning when the sheriff had come to Esteban's door, his soul had been touched by shadows.

Rather than seek the miracle of marital bliss a second time, Esteban chose to focus his attentions on his farm, and on his lovely daughter, Angelina. The love between father and daughter was so strong that, after Angelina earned her business degree at a college in Portland, she passed up the big glass buildings of that city in order to return to the farm and keep her father's books. Doubly blessed by his daughter's business sense and his ability to speak with his migrant workers in their native tongue, Esteban built the most successful family-owned orchard in the valley. The old man's happiness knew no bounds.

Intent on keeping their jobs with such an excellent and kind boss, the farmworkers took note of the bond between father and daughter and drew in any thoughts about Angelina. There was one, however, who had more trouble with this task than most.

Pedro Poncilla had arrived at the farm ten years before – in fact, soon after the death of the boss's wife. He was an illegal immigrant from Guadalajara with a sharp mind and a great desire to prove himself as a worker. He was profoundly moved by the grief he saw in the farmowner's eyes, and resolved to care for the orchards as if they were his own.

Even through the fog of his loss, Esteban Ochoas knew a remarkable young man when he saw one. He rewarded Pedro's unfailing labor by helping him obtain a green card, and then his American citizenship, and, finally, by promoting him to the job of foreman. Pedro thus became one of three workers who remained on the farm year-round, in a clean little cottage next to the south orchard.

From his front window, Pedro could look across the front lot of the farm and see the large window of Angelina's office, where she sat late at night reviewing the farm's paperwork. This ready vantage of the prize he could not have – her pillowed lips, cave-dark eyes, hair that shone like blackbird's wings – was not particularly good for Pedro's health.

Five years into his torment, Pedro thought about leaving. He could always hide his real reasons by making up some fib about an ailing grandmother in San Bernardino. He was soon granted a reprieve, however, in the person of Gustavo, a bespectacled migrante who was always spending his breaks and lunches with his nose buried in a book. Curious, Pedro asked Gustavo what was so compelling about these books. Gustavo handed him the volume he was reading just then – a collection of poetry by a man named Miguel Hernandez – and said, "Why don't you read this, and then you can tell me."

Reading at his front window that night, the halo'd vision of Angelina across the yard, Pedro could not believe the things that he discovered in the pages of Gustavo's book. Why, these were not normal Spanish words at all – they were like tropical birds the colors of Christmas ornaments, scrambling around in his head and taking him to wild, impossible landscapes. And all the next day, working in the orchards, the words of Miguel Hernandez continued to burn in his limbs, investing every small action with the goldenrod aura of new knowledge.

After consuming the dozen volumes in Gustavo's collection, Pedro took off each Saturday morning to pedal his squeaky old bike to the biblioteca in Hood River and gather more: Cesar Vallejo, Juan Ramon Jimenez, Una Muno, Octavio Paz, Pablo Neruda, and Gabriel Garcia Marquez. Soon enough, Pedro found that he, too, carried the poetic impulse, that he, too, could make his language fly like birds – though at lower altitudes, and with feathers much plainer. Still, he found that he could use his rough new skills as a way to tap off his irresolvable feelings about Angelina. He found a café near the biblioteca where he could spend hours reading his latest discovery and then translating that same sort of magic into his own writing, filling notebook after notebook with tributes to forbidden love.

Alas! Just about the time that Pedro had come to terms with his plight, he left the café one Saturday to discover Angelina's red truck parked across the street in front of the grocery store. The following week, he noticed the truck's arrival, and all the next month he made a study of Angelina's deeply entrenched routine. She would park outside the grocery just before eleven, walk down the street to do various errands, and then return at about one o'clock to do her grocery shopping.

This two-hour window was too much for Pedro to ignore, for here lay the opportunity to express his love directly, and yet maintain his anonymity. He would arrive in town at ten o'clock and carefully lock his bicycle out of sight, next to a tree behind the café. At noon, he would go next door to the florist shop, where a kindly old Anglo woman named Mabel would sell him a single blossom - a carnation one week, a rose the next, always changing. Then, while Angelina was off doing her errands, he would walk as casually as possible across the street to clip the flower under the driver's side windshield wiper on Angelina's truck.

He was too afraid to observe Angelina's return (the delivery itself made his strong workman's hands shake with anxiety), but that night, Angelina would turn on the lights in her office to reveal a small yellow vase on her desk – and in the vase, Pedro's flower!

This went on for a year, and still Pedro would feel a thrill when he spied his flowers on Angelina's window, still his hands would shake like a teenage vandal's when he made his deliveries. Eventually, however, even this was not enough to quell Pedro's longings, and once again he began to consider leaving the farm. This time, he had a concrete offer, a cousin at an apple orchard across the river in Washington who said he could get him a job whenever he wanted.

Pedro awoke one Saturday morning in early March to find the sky over Mount Hood like a perfect oil painting of cerulean blue. The orchards outside his bedroom window had just, in the previous eight hours, achieved the peak of their blossoming, a hazy field of snow-white flowers dripping here and there like the tears of angels.

Pedaling toward Hood River through this paradise, Pedro felt strangely overwhelmed. When he arrived at the café he wrote a poem about a man who camped out in a pear orchard. The man bedded down beneath a bower of blossoming pear branches, and in the morning a crew of workers discovered him dead, having literally asphyxiated himself in a pile of white petals.

At the florist's shop, Mabel (who had long ago figured out the object of Pedro's purchases) presented him with a white orchid, the most beautiful flower Pedro had ever seen. She sold it to him at a price that was much lower, he was sure, than its real cost. Still, even with the thought of the lovely orchid that would appear that evening in Angelina's window, he returned to the café feeling like a condemned man. He composed poem after poem about men killed by the terrorizing forces of beauty: a hunter clawed to death by an eagle with feathers of gold, an Alaskan explorer struck by a bolt of lightning from the heart of the Northern Lights, a teenaged boy so distracted by a passing bonita that he walks into the path of a speeding bus.

Two hours later, Pedro applied a final period to this gorgeous genocide, slapped his notebook shut and trudged from the café, too weighed down to even say goodbye to his pals Louis and Jake, hunched over their daily chess match. At the very moment of dropping down that last dot of ink, in fact, Pedro had resolved never to write a poem again. Once he escaped to the apple-fields of the north, he knew that the magic of words would conjure up Angelina's face at every stanza. His determination was so concrete, in fact, that he left behind a volume of poems by Federico Garcia Lorca atop his usual windowside table.

So it was that, with heart and feet turning steadily to iron, Pedro Poncilla rounded the back corner of the café to find a most unusual sight: his old bicycle, angled against the tree, covered from handlebar to rear fender in pear blossoms, whole branches of them, fixed to its metallic limbs with loops of white ribbon. It looked like a kind of two-wheeled float, dressed up for an Easter parade.

Frozen in place in the alleyway, Pedro could feel the beauty that had always been outside of him, now asphyxiating him, filling his lungs and mouth and muscles, inflating him to a man three times his former size. He knelt next to his bicycle, running his hands over its new tissue-paper skin, then untied the branches one by one, wrapping them in a sheet of butcher paper he got from Mabel. He tied the bundle to the center rod of his bicycle, and carefully placed the ribbons in his pocket. Then he rode home like a demon, questions flashing through his mind like the sparrows whipping past him in the wind.

He pulled into the farm to find father and daughter Ochoas standing next to the red truck, beaming in amusement and admiration, Angelina holding the white orchid in her hands. As Pedro pulled to a stop in the loose gravel of the drive, he could feel the tug of one last anxiety: how in the world could he explain himself? His concerns were shattered by the booming laughter of his boss.

"Señor Poncilla!" he shouted. "I see you have brought us more pear blossoms. I am so relieved; I was afraid we were going to run out!"

Esteban Ochoas stepped to Pedro's side and gave him a warm handshake. "I was wondering, Señor Poncilla, if you would do us the honor of having dinner tonight with my daughter and myself. I would like to discuss your apparently great interest in floral horticulture."

Pedro smiled shyly, afraid to look at Angelina's face lest it cause his heart to burst.He caught his breath and said, "Yes, by all means, Señor Ochoas. I… I would be honored. Yes."

"Do everything in your power and will to avoid sounding and writing like anyone else."

--Mike McGee, performance poet

Gooroo (Chekhov)

On the night of my freedom
a Cherokee barnowl spins by
to snatch my breath
a single helium balloon wanders the parking lot
like a security guard
and the soccer field is framed by airline seats

The history of drama is such that
no sane person would dare attempt it

("In her eyes, she is quiet, like a fish")

Better to climb the mountains on Lake Michigan
ski slaloms across Death Valley
eat ice cream with no apology

than try to wrap up the human bloodflow
like a fifty-cent candy bar

("You have created an elaborate romance for yourself")

Go find your answers in a bookstore
where they are rolling in Hemingway
on a handtruck

But tonight I will toss my every essential
into a hatchback
and just leave

Because leaving is the only response

In the Now

A fiction writer confesses his new-found love for writing in the present tense. Here's why you may want to consider bringing your own fiction into the present.

First published in Writer's Digest

For years, I've been fighting off the present tense.

I don't mean this as some Buddhist confession. I mean that, during the past twenty years, as literary novels began bursting forth with *he says, she walks* and *they dance*, I refused to participate. As a staunch minimalist, firmly opposed to anything that muddies the author/reader connection, I saw present-tense narrative as a showy, intrusive gimmick – and vowed my fealty to the great past-tense tradition.

Boy, was I due for a comeuppance.

During a holiday visit, I ransacked my sister's bookshelves and picked up *Blue Diary*, Alice Hoffman's 2001 novel about a small-town hero with a dark past. I finished a few days later, and was rereading the last page when I noticed it was written in past tense. Along with the 282 pages before it.

So much for "intrusive." And now I was curious. I took a short story that I'd been percolating – a man who falls in love with a barista who makes perfect lattes – and gave it a shot. Though I often lapsed into past tense (a 20-year habit is hard to kick), I found the transition remarkably seamless. I also found that the new tense imbued my descriptive passages with a poetic, gem-like quality. Rather than trying to describe this quality in precise terms, I'll give you a sample:

> *That night, Andre crosses his front lawn, huffing steam into the cold air. He pauses and sets down his guitar case. A full moon is filtering the madrone, silvering its smooth limbs. Reminding Andre*

of Roxanne's shoulders, bare and slender, turning away as the espresso bites into his tongue.

I am now halfway through my first present-tense novel, and have become the most unbearable of evangelists (like your Uncle Ralph, who finally quit smoking after 30 years, and wants to make sure everybody else does the same). So find a comfy spot on the pew as I bear witness to the present tense and its several salvations.

Putting the Reader Into the Story

If you watch the History Channel, you'll notice that most of its commentators speak in the present tense ("So there's Napolean, stuck behind enemy lines, and he's completely out of croissants!"). If you watch Comedy Central, you'll notice that the classic joke style is present tense ("Two authors walk into a bar..."). In both cases, the object is the same: to draw the listener into the center of the action.

Not that past tense prevents this. We are programmed by centuries of storytelling to take a past event and convert it to a present image. But if present tense can increase the efficiency of this mental conversion even five percent, why not use it?

Narrator Knowledge

One of the best ways to create power within a narrative is to pique the reader's interest by withholding information (for instance, a character who suffers extreme panic attacks but refuses to say what might be causing them). When you reveal these explanatory secrets later, you create a sense of resolution similar to the moment, in music, when a dissonant chord returns to its home key. In this way, all good books, no matter what their genre, are mysteries.

The past-tense narrative, however, implies that the events in a story have already occurred. It's easy for a reader to feel, therefore, that the secrets of the story are being withheld – and that he is being toyed with. Using present tense, the author creates the illusion that these events are unrolling at precisely the moment the reader is reading them – and that the narrator himself has no idea what's coming next. (All stories are manipulations, of course, but some are more subtle than others.)

Character Denotation

A few years ago, I wrote a novel featuring three first-person male narrators, and decided to give each of them a distinct manner of speaking. The shy artist used simple words and brief sentences. The cynical journalist used large words and complex sentences. The gregarious former jock spoke in present tense.

We all know this guy. He's loud, street-smart, and he loves to tell stories: "So Charlie and me, we're walkin' in there like we know what we're doin', and all of a sudden the fire sprinklers go off!"

Another present-speaker is the American teenager: "And then Suzanne goes, 'No way!' And I'm all, 'You have got to be kidding.' Then Terry pulls up in his Nissan and we're like, "Si-i-ck!'"

I make fun – and certainly no writer wants to work in stereotypes. But present-tense speaking contains a definite blue-collar undertone, and can come in handy for giving your character an immediate and recognizable style.

Killing the Pluperfect

For the geek grammarians and lovers of syntax, I save the best for last. I'm basically a musical writer, and I can't be happy with a sentence or paragraph unless it slides into a certain rhythmic track. One villain that continually messes with my mojo is the verb form that we call pluperfect.

A pluperfect phrase is formed by the word *had* and the past participle form of a verb (swim swam *swum*, get got *gotten*, drink drank *drunk*). "Johnny *had swum* across the lake, where he *had drunk* too much and *had gotten* sick." Put simply, pluperfect describes an event that happened before a past-tense event. (The equivalent form in adjectives would be the superlative: close, closer, *closest*.)

In a past-tense narrative, the author is operating on two primary levels. The main thrust of the story occurs in the past tense; flashbacks and recollections take place in pluperfect. Especially in tales where memory plays an important role, the author will spend a lot of time dealing with those clunky *had gottens* and *had swums*.

By using the present tense as his base, the author is able to handle past events in past tense (an enormously logical concept) and rid himself of pluperfect. Even better, he can keep pluperfect in his back pocket, in case he needs to describe an event that occurs *before* a flashback or recollection. He has just expanded his arsenal of tense from two to three (or, if you include future tense – *will swim* – from three to four).

To illustrate, I'll take a passage from my novel and mess with it. First, its current form. Note how neatly the tense switches from past to present.

My memories of Tuesday are like figures viewed through marble glass, but a few odd tracks are clear. Nefertiti found an excuse for buying me a drink – then, arriving at a busy café, instructed me to save a table while she got the cappuccinos. She sprinkled hers with chocolate; she sprinkled mine with Ecstasy.

Now, I'll convert the same passage to past and pluperfect.

My memories of Tuesday were like figures viewed through marbled glass, but a few odd tracks were clear. Nefertiti *had found* an excuse for buying me a drink – then, arriving at a busy café, *had instructed* me to save a table while she *had gotten* the cappuccinos. She *had sprinkled* hers with chocolate; she *had sprinkled* mine with Ecstasy.

Admittedly, the switch in no way destroys the passage. But you can feel the rhythmic dissonance. Extend this over a 300-page novel and the difference is enormous. (Worse yet, imagine an entire novel composed in pluperfect!)

It's no accident that poets – working in the most rhythmically demanding form of all – are particularly fond of present tense.

Why Not?

Unlike your Uncle Ralph and his cigarettes, I would never completely forsake the past tense (you'll note that I used it for this article). But from now on, the present tense will hold a special place in my repertoire.

The truth is, if the author does his work, the average reader won't even notice. So pick what's best for you – what's best for your story – and have at it.

In researching this article, I was ransacking another bookcase – belonging to my friend Anne – for present-tense novels.

Oh, wait a minute. Let's do this in present tense.

So I'm pulling out Myla Goldberg's *Bee Season* – a 2000 bestseller about spelling bees – and Anne says, "Oh, that's really good – but it's not in present tense."

I scan a few random pages, take a quick survey of verbs, and say, "Wanna bet?"

Master Class, Licia Albanese, February 21, 1998

Who's going to drink this water?
Certainly not me

You're not scared of the audience
You're scared of me

Give life to the words
Every word needs a life

Make the last note long
That way, the people will know you're finished

When you get to the top note, I will give you a pinch so you make it
this time

Walk, walk
That way you don't get tense while you're singing

This is opera
You have to give to them
so they come back
to hear you

Don't rush – this is Puccini!
Wait! Wait!

I didn't believe you could sìng this, because your voice is fortissimo
But it's good

This is the way I want you all to sing

Why Meter Matters

First published in Writer's Digest

The 20th century was not particularly kind to metered verse. This was partly because, at the end of the 19th century, a group of French poets declared the birth of *vers libre*, or "free verse," which sought to shake off the strictures of traditional poetry and pursue the more natural rhythms of common speech. With precedents like the Psalms of the King James Bible and Walt Whitman's 1855 *Leaves of Grass*, plus new English-language champions like Ezra Pound and T.S. Eliot, free verse performed so well that, today, it is absolutely the dominant form. In 2006, the only way to get metered verse published is through specialized journals, children's books, or by being an already-famous poet.

So why bother with meter at all? Because, in its methodical, technically demanding fashion, it helps us to better understand and manipulate the rhythms of language. It's much like a jazz musician, who can improvise much more readily if he first learns the age-old chord structures of classical music.

Getting to Know Your Feet

The subatomic particle of meter is the foot – the two or three syllables that make up the "beat" in a line of verse.

Iamb: a weak syllable followed by a strong syllable. "To *be* / or *not* / to *be*…" (Shakespeare)

Trochee: a strong syllable followed by a weak syllable. "*Ty*ger! / *Ty*ger! / *bur*ning / *bright*…" (William Blake)

Dactyl: a strong syllable followed by two weak syllables. "*This* is the / *for*est pri- / *me*val…" (Longfellow)

Anapest: two weak syllables followed by a strong syllable. "I am *lord* / of the *fowl* / and the *brute*." (Robert Frost)

Placekeepers: Occasional appearances are made by the *Spondee* (two strong syllables) and the *Pyrrhic* (two weak syllables) - but if you tried to base an entire poem on either one of these, your head would explode.

Building the House

Now that you've got your feet, let's get walking. Try a few of the following forms for yourself – but *please note:* the idea is not to obsessively follow a chosen footstyle, but to use it as a general structure. As long as you maintain the integrity of your "beats," occasional deviations are not only permissible – they tend to add interest.

Iambic Pentameter

Five iambic feet (weak-strong) per line

Although it's easy to credit Chaucer, Shakespeare and Milton for immortalizing this Godfather of Verse, at heart it's the heartbeat (ba-*dum*, ba-*dum*) and a prime-number, indivisible flow of beats that produces a smooth, circular feel (think "Take Five" by Dave Brubeck). It's also surprisingly common in everday speech, as in the phrase, "I'd like a decaf mocha frappuccino." Write it in non-rhyming "blank" verse – as Shakespeare did in his plays – or try out the classic sonnet form: fourteen lines in two parts, the octave (eight lines) and the sestet (six lines). Then sing it to the tune of "Danny Boy."

"But if the while I think on thee, dear friend…" (Shakespeare)

Common Meter

Alternating lines of iambic tetrameter (four beats) and iambic trimeter (three beats)

The favored meter of Emily Dickinson – and yes, you can sing it to the tune of "Gilligan's Island" (or, for that matter, "The Beverly Hillbillies").

"Because I could not stop for Death,
He kindly stopped for me…"
(Dickinson)

Dactyllic Ballad

The same alternating four- and three-beat lines as Common Meter,
but using the dactyllic foot (strong-weak-weak), which lends the
poem a galloping, waltz-like rhythm.

"Frederick and Daisy are crazy for me,
but frankly I question their taste…"
(Vaughn)

Trochaic Octameter

Eight trochaic feet (strong-weak) per line

Try it to the tune of "Hark the Herald Angels Sing."

"Once upon a midnight dreary, while I pondered, weak and
weary…" (Edgar Allan Poe)

Limerick

A five-line anapestic poem (weak-weak-strong) in which lines 1, 2
and 5 have three beats and a rhyme, while lines 3 and 4 have two
beats and a rhyme.

"A man with a chest cold named Bill
Ingested a nuclear pill.
The doctor said 'cough,'
The damn thing went off,
And they picked up Bill's head in Brazil."
(Anon.)

Make Up Your Own

Like any good cook, once you know all the ingredients – footstyle, number of beats per line, number of lines per stanza – it's time to start mixing things up, leaning on your innate sense of rhythm to tell you whether or not something "clicks in."

Years ago, I wrote a parody cowboy poem called "And Roy Rogers Sang the Torah." I didn't realize until much later that I had been writing in lines of trochaic heptameter (seven beats of strong-weak) centered on a fourth pyrrhic foot (weak-weak) that acted as a pause, or "caesura."

"North we go a-roaming from Wyoming to Montana,
all upon a tankful of George Custer's diesel gas…"

If someone had actually *instructed* me to write in that particular scheme, I'd still be there now, a-staring at the page.

What is the single biggest mistake that poets make in marketing their work?

"Paying too much attention to marketing their work."

--Jane Hirshfield, poet

Melisma

Destroyed by autumn leaves
Christmas songs mid-November
wondering if we can cram any more death
into one year

I am constantly walking into photographs
Someday I will hire a detective to
track them down, demand royalties

Why is everyone in the café so obnoxious?
Has there been a release?

I wish singers
would learn to sing
with less emotion

Canadian guitars
winging a vee across the narrows
looking for one true voice

You don't need to be good.
You need to mean it.

"People gravitate toward fiction to better understand the facts"

--David Baldacci

Anatomy of a Bestseller

What do the novels *Life of Pi, Bridget Jones's Diary* and *The Rule of Four* have in common? You might be surprised. Learn how to apply the techniques and traits they share to your own writing.

First published in Writer's Digest

If anyone tells you he has a sure-fire formula for a bestseller, quickly back away and keep one hand on your wallet. There are simply too many radical factors in the success of a novel: demographic quirks, talk-show endorsements, marketing expenditures, distribution deals …

And constant surprises. Go back 10 years and imagine hearing this: "In the next decade, the publishing industry will be conquered by a 14-year-old murder victim narrating from heaven, a cryptologist uncovering church secrets in Renaissance paintings and millions of kids lining up to read a 900-page book about a teenage wizard." (*That's The Lovely Bones, The Da Vinci Code* and—come on! Where have you been?)

Still, although it's nigh-on impossible to mimic your way onto the bestseller list, you'd be a fool to pass up all the secrets to be found in successful, well-written books. Let's take a vastly divergent trio of recent hits—*Bridget Jones's Diary, The Rule of Four* and *Life of Pi*—and see what they have in common.

Make Promises

In *The Rule of Four*, two Princeton students search a Renaissance text, the *Hypnerotomachia Poliphili*, for startling secrets. Narrator Tom Sullivan begins by describing the execution of two untrustworthy Renaissance messengers. He goes on:

Five hundred years would elapse before anyone discovered the truth. When those five centuries passed, and death found a new pair of messengers, I was finishing my last year of college at Princeton.

Co-authors Ian Caldwell and Dustin Thomason have just struck a bargain with the reader: *We know that Renaissance text analysis sounds like a dry subject—but people are going to die over this!* And so the reader turns the page.

In *Life of Pi*, the promise arrives in the form of simple geography. Author Yann Martel's protagonist lies in a Mexican hospital bed, suffering from severe symptoms of exposure. But his narrative begins with his childhood in India. What happened between India and Mexico? You have to keep reading to find out.

Bridget Jones begins her *Diary* with a list of New Year's resolutions, revealing the cockeyed self-delusion that will fuel the rest of the story:

I will ... develop inner poise and authority and sense of self as a woman of substance complete without boyfriend, as best way to obtain boyfriend.

The promise here is simple: You *will* have fun.

You don't need "Call me Ishmael." You don't need a boulder chasing Indiana Jones from the cave. But you do need to deliver an intriguing promise, and you need to keep it.

The Pistol on the Mantelpiece

One of the oldest saws of the theater world decrees that, should you place a pistol on the mantelpiece, then sometime before the final curtain, someone had better shoot it. Otherwise, you're creating an expectation and failing to fulfill it.

Early in *Life of Pi*, the eponymous narrator spends an entire chapter explaining the psychological underpinnings of lion taming. Granted, Pi is the son of a zookeeper, but this would still seem a frivolous digression—if not for the fact that he eventually finds himself trapped on a lifeboat with a Bengal tiger.

In *The Rule of Four*, the boys of Princeton spend Chapter 2 playing laser tag in a network of steam tunnels underneath the campus. How disappointing would it be, in a thriller filled with chase scenes, if those dangerous, alluring tunnels failed to make a reappearance?

Now for the bonus round. When Bridget Jones first encounters impressive lawyer Mark Darcy, she takes one look at his awful holiday sweater (the kind "favored by the more elderly of the nation's sports reporters") and immediately writes him off. When he reappears 80 pages later, sans sweater and suddenly quite appealing, it not only legitimizes that early appearance, but it allows any reader who's caught on to Bridget's extraordinarily bad judgment to declare, "Aha! I knew it!" And the stage is set to watch this seemingly minor character become a prime mover in the rest of the book.

Lingo Bonding

As teenagers, we learn to solidify our circle of friends through the use of slang and syntax. In much the same way, authors can build relationships with their readers. For instance, the odd sentence structures of E. Annie Proulx's *Shipping News* or the minimalist punctuation of Cormac McCarthy's *All the Pretty Horses* may initially be off-putting. But once the reader adjusts to it—once he becomes part of the "inner circle"—he'll not only finish the book, but he'll get into bar fights defending the author's good name.

Bridget Jones owes much of her fame to author Helen Fielding's wickedly funny use of language. By combining artful abbreviation (v.g. for "very good"), pronoun-free diaryspeak ("Understand where have been going wrong …") and entries reflecting the protagonist's immediate state of mind ("Course is OK—everyone drunks office Christmas parties"), the *Diary* inspired a veritable army of single, female copycats.

In *The Rule of Four*, language is entirely the point. Our scholars are spelunkers of meaning, making their way through the treacherous caverns of the *Hypnerotomachia* armed with Latin wordplay, cryptological ciphers and numerical analyses. It's an enormous treat for bibliophiles that's mapped out by the authors with an astonishing clarity.

Pi Patel narrates his *Life* with the formalized English of India and a poet's heart: "It is pointless to say that this or that night was the worst of my life. I have so many bad nights to choose from that I've made none the champion."

Much of Martel's wordplay is actually nameplay. The hero is named Piscine, after the French word for "swimming pool." He later changes it to Pi, after the mathematical figure. His two favorite teachers—an atheist biologist and a Muslim baker—are both named Kumar. And for 40 pages, the oft-mentioned Richard Parker appears to be human—until a tiger with that name climbs into Pi's lifeboat. All of these names have their stories, all are rich in symbolism and all drive the plot forward.

Crank It Up

Are you giving your hero a hard time? Good! Adversity is the most essential spice in the fiction chef's pantry. Just when things look their bleakest, however, stop and ask yourself this question: How can I make it even worse?

Halfway through her *Diary*, Bridget pops up to the roof of boyfriend Daniel's flat to discover a naked, blonde Amazon named Suki. A week later, Bridget accepts Daniel's fervent invitation to drinks, expecting a plea for forgiveness and reunion. But here's what he says: "The thing is, Suki and I … we're getting married."

After struggling through the death of a colleague, mind-numbing riddles and accusations of plagiarism from theft-minded superiors, *The Rule of Four*'s Tom and Paul finally decode the passage that should contain the Big Secret—only to run into a big fat "however." Their Renaissance puzzler has lost his nerve, deposited the real secrets in the *Hypnerotomachia*'s second half and told them, in essence, you're on your own. ("Only your intellect will guide you now.")

In a sense, the entire narrative of *Life of Pi* is "cranking it up." On the third day of his lifeboat odyssey, Pi is understandably preoccupied by the dangerous face-off between a hyena and an orangutan, over the dying body of a zebra. He hasn't seen the tiger since the sinking of the ship and has begun to think the whole thing was an illusion. But when the hyena kills the orangutan (a creature Pi had known since childhood), Pi becomes enraged and steps to the "animal" side of the lifeboat to attack the hyena. It's at this point that he spies the huge head of Richard Parker, who's been hiding under a tarp, plagued with seasickness. "You might think I lost all hope at that point," he says. "I did."

Mess with People's Beliefs

After the sensation caused by Dan Brown's *The Da Vinci Code* (whose take on church history held the feet of Catholicism to the fire), it's clear that challenging long-held beliefs is an excellent way to sell books. And it always has been. Consider *The Satanic Verses*, *Fear of Flying*, *On the Road*, *Catcher in the Rye*, *The Grapes of Wrath*, *The Jungle* and *Uncle Tom's Cabin*.

With its Renaissance scholarship and revisions of history, *The Rule of Four* may seem merely a *Da Vinci Code* knockoff, but by all accounts, it's just a happy coincidence. Caldwell and Thomason began their book years before *Da Vinci Code*'s release and wrote it in a much different style. Regardless, *Rule of Four*'s Medici-era showdown between secular art and religious morality makes for provocative reading on its premise alone.

The beach read *Bridget Jones's Diary* actually asks a semiserious and topical question: Is the single life really so bad, or is it more the hell-on-earth created by the expectations of society, family and the "Smug Marrieds"? Bridget coins a name for aging free agents like herself ("Singletons") and asks the rest of the world to please leave them bloody well alone.

Life of Pi takes on beliefs at every step, beginning with religion. As a teenager, Pi decides to practice the Christian, Hindu and Muslim faiths all at the same time, and manages to plead a pretty good case for why this isn't the problem it appears to be on the surface. (Though he cringes when his three spiritual advisers and his modern, secular parents all find out about one another's existence at once, and in person.) Pi also expresses surprising admiration for atheists—

"my brothers and sisters of a different faith"—whom he prefers to ever-doubting agnostics.

On a smaller scale, Pi offers a compelling argument in favor of zoos, which, he argues, provide a much better existence for wildlife than the parasite- and predator-infested wilderness.

Attention to Detail

It's a little too easy to brush aside comic works like *Bridget Jones's Diary*, when, in fact, any honest writer who's tried it will tell you that comedy is the hardest genre of all. But Fielding produced much more than a few laughs; she created a fully drawn, exquisitely flawed heroine who seems to reflect the experiences of millions of women around the globe. Fielding developed Bridget as the star of a regular column in a British news-paper, *The Independent*, and this gradual evolution obviously helped in working out the details. It's Bridget's humanity, her ability to elicit an, "Oh my god, I do that, too!" response in the reader, that allowed Fielding to launch an entire new genre of fiction (that would be chick lit) with this one book.

The tiger-in-a-lifeboat premise of *Life of Pi* is so outrageous that only excruciating attention to detail could make it plausible. Be it a description of a sea turtle's flipper, the changing colors of a dorado fish as it fights its own death or the inventory list of a lifeboat's supply locker, Martel battles the incredulity of his primary conflict with the eye of a hyper-realist.

Pi also brings up another option for fiction writers: investing your story with a peripheral body of knowledge, again, through interesting details. Pi's small lectures on theology and zoology (beginning with a treatise on two- and three-toed sloths) enrich the reader's knowledge of his background as Pi prepares to relate his great adventure.

The Rule of Four's peripheral body of knowledge is an entire—and actual—book, providing its authors an opportunity to lay before the reader a hearty meal of Renaissance culture and history. Caldwell and Thomason spent six years researching and writing their book. I'm betting that the scenes they had the least trouble imagining were the ones in which Tom and Paul leave the library stacks after hours of eye-glazing, mind-numbing research into the *Hypnerotomachia*.

If you take anything away from this session of idea-harvesting, take this: You'll save yourself a lot of trouble if you take on a subject you're passionate about. The work will seem like joy, the joy will radiate from the page and perhaps, someday, you'll find your name on that precious list of bestsellers. And people will steal ideas from you.

Exercises

Make Promises
After you write the earth-shattering climax of Chapter 21, go back to those first few pages of your novel and see if there are places where you can insert tantalizing hints of things to come.

The Pistol on the Mantelpiece
Uh-oh. Something just popped into your story, and you have no idea what it means. (This happened to me when one of my characters, in a frantic inner monologue, suddenly mentioned "poor Stephanie.") Should it stay or go? Take a shot at writing an explanation for its appearance and how it might effect your plot. Ten chapters later in my book, Stephanie ended up serving as the catalyst for the novel's primary climax.

Lingo Bonding
If a character in your novel has an unusual name, devise a story to explain it. I once had a protagonist named Scootie. No particular reason—it just dropped into my head—but a friend demanded that I explain myself. Turns out Scootie's real name was Leonard, but he got a middle-ear infection as a baby and began crawling sideways like a crab. The story became a running joke in the novel.

Crank It Up
Got your hero pinned to the mat? Stop right there, take out a piece of paper and write 10 ways you could make the situation even worse. You may decide to use none of them. But one of them could be just the twist to make your story unforgettable.

Mess With People's Beliefs

When considering issues you'd like to take on in your fiction, think about the ones you're not decisive about. Gray areas produce much more interesting—and surprising—outcomes than black-and-white absolutes. Better yet, think of an issue that few people would disagree on (um, "thou shalt not run with scissors"?), and think of a scenario in which you could argue the opposite view.

Attention to Detail

At the beginning of your novel-writing process, consider your characters' hobbies or backgrounds, and do a little research on those subjects. Such knowledge can deepen your story. For my current novel, which stars a geneticist, I found scientific studies that connected directly with my main storyline—a tale of divorce and adultery—which I hadn't realized had scientific corollaries.

Harold in Motion

Only in black-and-white movies or the
Crow's Nest in Santa Cruz does the crowd form a
ring around the lead couple but my
dad is spinning it old-school, jitterbugging my
stepmom across the parquet.

A 73-year-old has no business looking so
smooth, backbone lanked-out like a fifties bopper,
head forward he scratches a couple of chicken-steps,
kick-starts a Harley and swoops an Elvis tune,
hands a pair of six-shooters at his side he
flips his partner into a spin like he's handing her off to
someone else who turns out to be himself.

Ask a 73-year-old why he pumps weights and
jogs a chocolate poodle down a beach while his
peers melt into couches countrywide; he'll say,
For a group of absolute strangers who will
yell him through fifty-year-old steps from an
Indiana dance hall, then slap him on the back as he
retreats to his table, Jailhouse Rock echoing in his ears.

Somewhere in my near future I will pull a
breathless redhead out of a dip and she'll say,
Wow! You sure can dance.
Oh yeah? says I. You oughta see my old man.

Dashboard Dvorak

In the novel *Operaville*, opera blogger Mickey Siskel finds himself
in the otherworldly position of nursing his favorite diva, Maddalena
Hart, through an anxiety attack. Two days later, having successfully
restored her confidence, he tells the story of how he became such a
passionate aficionado of the form.

There's a third cabin on the property, but it's hardly ever occupied.
Apparently, it's being rented by people who never vacation. The
previous renter assembled a fire pit, using stones salvaged from the
nearby woods. Maddie and I sit on a log, caretakers of a vigorous
blaze, doing our best to roast marshmallows on the tips of bouncy
coat-hanger rods. I consume my latest victim - blessed with a suntan
worthy of a bikini model – and I decide that it's time to 'fess up.

"May I tell you my story?"

"I expected you might," she says, and takes my hand. "I give you the
downbeat."

I steer a ship's-captain gaze over the flames to find my subject, a
third up from the horizon, three percent on the wane, a wisp of cloud
crossing its beacon.

I didn't have much of a calling, but I went to college during the
Reagan era, so I ended up in business school. Finance. I was a very
social creature – president of my frat, an athlete, not unattractive. My
guidance counselor said, You're good with people – go into stocks.
You'll be good with the clients.

So I did. Didn't even need a master's. He was right, I *was* good, and
it was certainly the right time to get in. Weathered the early-'90s
recession, got into tech stocks, surfed my way into the Clinton boom.
I married a co-worker, Allison – marvelous girl, beautiful, sexy,
smart as a whip. We bought a house in south San Jose, we were in
excellent shape. It was time to start a family.

We couldn't. Seven miscarriages. We got pregnant, but poor Allison couldn't hold them. She quit her job, thought that might help. It didn't.

Our reactions were a little cross-gender. Each of our miscarriages hit me like a steamroller. Deep depressions that lasted for weeks, couldn't even get out of bed unless I had to go to work. I saw each one as a real, living baby – a creature that poops its diapers and giggles when you make a face – so each one was, to me, a genuine, visceral death. Allison seemed wholly unaffected, as if these were not deaths but failures, part of a process. She wanted to try again, as soon as she was able, for as long as it took.

After seven, I couldn't do it any more. And neither one of us wanted to adopt. That might seem selfish, but I think it takes a certain kind of couple, with a certain mindset, to take that on. We were wise enough to know that we were not those people.

For a few years we went on as a childless couple. People do this, we said. People live fulfilling lives without children. I was always the wiz kid at the brokerage, always on the edge of things, so it was natural for me to get into derivatives. It was very creative. I was helping to invent entirely new ways to produce revenue; sometimes it felt like I was pulling cash out of the air. But a few years down the line, when the inventing part was over, I came to realize that what I was doing had no real value. I wasn't producing anything that was any good to society. I was only using this mathematical sleight-of-hand to make a stacked deck even more unfair, to make filthy rich people even richer.

I decided that I wanted out. With no children to provide for, and Allison back at her old job, I thought I deserved a little time to lift my nose from the grindstone. I met Colin at a barbecue. He told me that he was starting a deck-staining business and needed an assistant. I had always done all the work on our house myself – including painting the exterior and staining the deck – and, in fact, had found it to be excellent therapy. So I took Colin's card.

Allison didn't like it. She wanted us to be a power couple; she wanted us to keep piling up money and play the games of the elite: Junior League, charity boards – maybe the opera. We fought for a month, non-stop, viciously, noisily. I'm surprised the cops never showed up. She called me a lazy, self-absorbed piece of shit. I called her a money-grubbing bitch.

I summarily quit my job and began working for Colin. I adored the work. I loved the ache in my muscles, the long, quiet hours, the spectacular views. There was even an element of voyeurism, getting to invade all these private spaces, to see how other people lived. And mostly, I loved the concrete-ness of the product. We took these graying, sun-baked, moss-covered wretches, cleaned them up, stained them over and made them into beautiful objects. I pictured our clients coming out for their morning coffee, seeing their shiny deck through the kitchen window and thinking, *Maybe I'll eat breakfast outside.*

As I got more into the business, I realized I needed a more appropriate vehicle. I bought my sister's station wagon. It had already suffered ten years of child abuse (so to speak), so I certainly didn't have to worry about being nice to it. For years, I kept discovering bits of its previous life: a Spiderman action figure under the passenger seat, a pack of bubble gum tucked under a seat cushion, an empty juice box next to the spare tire. The only thing I didn't like was that the stereo didn't work. But after hot days I was certainly grateful for the air conditioning.

Eventually I moved into an apartment. I let Allison have the house. But that wasn't enough. I learned from mutual friends that she intended to ruin me. She hired an expensive attorney and took everything: assets, bank accounts, my BMW. I have no idea why she deserved any of this, but it's amazing what a good lawyer can do. His most astounding move was to use the miscarriages as an example of the pain and suffering she had to undergo during the marriage. My lawyer (the big overpaid jagoff) had no answer for this. The settlement included alimony – alimony! – and I was soon on my way to bankruptcy. An *actual* bankruptcy, however, might have put an end to the bloodletting, so they left me barely enough money to live on. And to twist slowly in the wind.

The apartment was now too expensive, but Colin was moving out of his cabin and told me what a deal it was. I really wasn't sure about the location, but I was getting used to driving mountain roads, so I thought, What the hell. It seemed like a good time to get away from civilization. On a Sunday in July, I made a trip to the cabin and unloaded my first wagonful. When I got back in, the car wouldn't start. I checked the battery terminals, the wires, made sure the alternator belts were tight. I tried the ignition. Nothing. So there I am, beset by all these doubts about living in the woods, and already I'm stranded. As the full weight of this thought struck me – accompanied by the baseline depression I was already living with – I could feel the life force seeping from my limbs. It wasn't sadness, or anxiety – those carry a certain emotional vigor. This was me, an empty shell, nothing left. This was the bottom.

I sat there in the driver's seat for a long time, in something like a psychosomatic coma. Couldn't move, couldn't lift a hand, didn't have enough energy to swear. Allison had finally got me. I pictured her somewhere, holding a voodoo doll, gleefully raising a pin.

Some time later I noticed the fuse box, just behind the parking brake. I was just ignorant enough about cars to see this as a possibility. I slid off the cap, and behold! two fuses that appeared to be loose. I pressed them back into place and, holding on to the thinnest thread of hope, I cranked the ignition.

The engine did nothing. But the stereo came to life! And out of the speakers came this song of indescribable, ghostly mournfulness. I had no idea about the words – they sounded Slavic, maybe Hebrew – but I could hear the pleading, the unbearably beautiful sadness. And the voice. I had the usual pedestrian ideas about opera – that snooty thing that had nothing to do with real life. But this voice, this woman, was so much the opposite. The voice was big but intimate, confiding. *I've been there too*, she said. *I know how you feel.* I imagined her as the mother of my miscarried children.

Then the orchestra began to well up, and the woman's voice rose to these long, sustained notes. I felt the sound strike me at a point just beneath my eyes, and I sat there in my car, sobbing. A minute later, the woman sounded like she was pleading for her life, and then, suddenly, that was the end. Another song began, and I cranked the ignition, and it started!

I find Maddie trying to suppress a smile.

"'Song to the Moon?'"

"Sitting in that tape player, all those years, waiting for someone to reconnect that fuse."

"Me?"

"Yes."

She folds her hands beneath her chin.

"You know, sometimes I get this idea that what I do has no relevance to real life. Sort of like your derivatives. But then, someone tells me a story like that. But I never dreamed that I faith-healed a car!"

"Well," I say. "It turns out it was the starter. Apparently, before they completely die out, they can still work every fifth time or so."

"But only if you're playing the right aria."

"By the right singer. No. I don't give you complete credit for restarting the car. But you did restart *me*. In any case, I headed right up the hill, having no idea that I was driving to a tune called "Somber Forest," and I took it straight to my mechanic in Los Gatos. Colin was nice enough to give me an advance so I could get it fixed. All things considered, I remained at the low point of my life for perhaps ten minutes. So I guess I can't complain. You want another marshmallow?"

She gives me a close-lipped smile. "I want another kiss."

I'm 47, and I'm not dumb. I begin at the upper right-hand corner of those luscious petals and I work my way across, taking my time to dip my tongue in between. This will be no surprise to aficionados of opera, but Maddie is very talented with her tongue. Keep that in mind the next time you see *Rigoletto* and you hear Gilda whip out a really wicked rolled R. Ten minutes later, I finish with a kiss on the tip of her nose. She speaks without opening her eyes.

"So that's when you became obsessed with the opera."

"Yes. That's also when I dreamed up my devious, terribly involved plan to find the woman who sang that gorgeous aria and make out with her."

She opens her eyes just barely and gives me a grin. "You are *so* lucky it wasn't Joan Sutherland."

Apologia

Perhaps I had forgotten to tell you
why I do this
by the plate glass windows of the this coffeehouse
chairs stacked up on tables
and me out here on the steel railings
brushing down the deadbolt click of a
chapter's final word
the easy snap of a dictionary.

I need this
I need this more than
solid blue numbers in a checkbook
or a young girl's smile
or a cereal with fiber

Grant me one small brake on the
steady slip of time
a night-fed gap where teenagers
kick coffee cups around the parking lot
where tomorrow's mist hangs high
just across the road, patient as a hawk
and your thoughts settle down so heavy and warm
that your eyes cannot quite focus.

And so, if I had forgotten to tell you
that place, tonight
I was there
and my head rings with sound.

First published in The Eclectic Literary Forum